D1020074

PREJUDICE
IN CHILDREN

PREJUDICE IN CHILDREN

Edited by

ALAN R. BROWN, Ph.D.

Associate Professor and Clinical Psychologist
Department of Special Education
Arizona State University
Tempe, Arizona

CHARLES C THOMAS · PUBLISHER
Springfield · Illinois · U.S.A.

Published and Distributed Throughout the World by
CHARLES C THOMAS • PUBLISHER
BANNERSTONE HOUSE
301-327 East Lawrence Avenue, Springfield, Illinois, U.S.A.
NATCHEZ PLANTATION HOUSE
735 North Atlantic Boulevard, Fort Lauderdale, Florida, U.S.A.

© 1972, by CHARLES C THOMAS • PUBLISHER
ISBN 0-398-02247—X (cloth)
ISBN 0-398-02478—2 (paper)
Library of Congress Catalog Card Number: 73-169874

With THOMAS BOOKS careful attention is given to all details of
manufacturing and design. It is the Publisher's desire to present books
that are satisfactory as to their physical qualities and artistic possibilities
and appropriate for their particular use. THOMAS BOOKS will be true
to those laws of quality that assure a good name and good will.

Printed in the United States of America
HH-11

TO
LISA AND JENNIFER

WHAT A CHILD BELIEVES

Some beliefs are like pleasant gardens with high walls around them.
They encourage exclusiveness, and the feeling of being especially
   privileged.
Other beliefs are expansive and lead the way into wider and deeper
   sympathies.

Some beliefs are like shadows, darkening children's days with fears
   of unknown calamities.
Other beliefs are like the sunshine, blessing children with the warmth
   of happiness.

Some beliefs are divisive, separating the saved from the unsaved,
   friends from enemies.
Other beliefs are bonds in a universal brotherhood, where sincere
   differences beautify the pattern.

Some beliefs are like blinders, shutting off the power to choose one's
   own direction.
Other beliefs are like gateways opening up vistas of exploration.

Some beliefs weaken a child's selfhood. They blight the growth of
   resourcefulness.
Other beliefs nurture self-confidence and enrich the feeling of personal
   worth.

Some beliefs are rigid, like the body of death, impotent in a changing
   world.
Other beliefs are pliable, like the young sapling, ever growing with
   the upward thrust of life.

It is indeed important what mankind has believed.
It is important what we believe.
And what a child believes also is a serious matter—not a subject for
   jest or sentimentality.

AUTHOR UNKNOWN

PREFACE

Prejudice refers to both an unfounded judgment and a feeling-tone. When we speak of *negative* ethnic prejudice, we are referring to hostile attitudes, over-categorization, unwarranted judgments and rigidity. Perhaps the most clear and concise definition has been put forth by Gordon Allport in his comprehensive and penetrating study of the origin and nature of prejudice entitled "The Nature of Prejudice":

> Ethnic prejudice is an antipathy based upon a faulty and inflexible generalization. It may be felt or expressed. It may be directed toward a group as a whole, or toward an individual because he is a member of that group.
>
> The net effect . . . is to place the object of prejudice at some disadvantage not merited by his own misconduct.

This book of articles and research readings was compiled because of my interest in this phenomena and in the hope that with continued dissemination of our growing knowledge in the area of human relationships, application can reduce group tensions and that the attitudes, behavior and devastating thinking that make up prejudice can be modified.

Clearly this is one of our most, if not the most serious of social problems. This is true in our country and perhaps truer throughout most of the world. To continue to ignore this problem (as, relatively speaking, we have been doing) or to minimize it, is clearly to invite disaster.

Several people deserve a word of thanks for their assistance in putting this book together. Miss Kathy France took the major secretarial responsibility and worked diligently and conscientiously. I am grateful and appreciative also to Mrs. Ruth Browning who is our department "executive" secretary extraordinaire. My wife, Linda, offers continual support in any and all endeavors. This, in combination with her warmth, sensitivity and tolerance for people commands my affection and respect.

A. R. B.

CONTENTS

PREJUDICE
IN CHILDREN

Race awareness
beings at a young
age

I. CHILDREN'S AWARENESS OF ETHNIC DIFFERENCES AND THE DEVELOPMENT OF ATTITUDES

Chapter 1

RACIAL ACCEPTANCE AND PREFERENCE OF NURSERY SCHOOL CHILDREN IN A SOUTHERN CITY

J. KENNETH MORLAND

Randolph-Macon Woman's College
Lynchburg, Virginia

S tudies of race awareness in young children have consistently emphasized the importance of the *social milieu* in the development of such awareness.* The research on which this paper is based sought to throw more light on the relationship between "milieu" and "awareness" by finding out what perceptions of race were held by children in a highly segregated environment, where virtually no direct contact between children of different races takes place. The study was designed specifically to determine whether Negro and white nursery school children reared in a racially segregated community were willing to accept members of the other race as playmates and whether they had a preference for playmates of one race or the other.† The study also sought to discover if racial acceptance and preference were essentially the same for all of the

---

Note. Reprinted by permission from *Merrill-Palmer Quarterly of Behavior and Development*, Vol. 8, No. 4, 1962. This article was originally a revision of a paper read at the annual meeting of the American Sociological Association, St. Louis, Missouri, August 31, 1961. Grants from the University Center in Virginia, Randolph-Macon Woman's College, and the Southern Fellowships Fund helped to make the study possible and are gratefully acknowledged.

*Most of these studies[5,7,12,16,17] deal with children in integrated schools. In the author's opinion, it is important to study the perception of race held by children in a racially segregated environment, while such environments still exist.

†An earlier report on the community[8] dealt with racial recognition ability, and reported that white children in a racially segregated city were able to distinguish between Negro and white at a significantly earlier age than Negro children. In contrast, studies in integrated schools of Massachusetts[5] and New York[7] had found that

subjects, or whether there was variation by age, race, racial recognition ability, and social status. Finally, a purpose of the study was to see if preference for playmates of one race was accompanied by the rejection of playmates of the other race when no choice was involved.*

METHOD

Setting

The research was carried out over a four-year period beginning in 1957 in Lynchburg, Virginia, a city of some 55,000 persons of whom 11,000, or 20 percent, are Negroes. During the time of the study, Lynchburg maintained strict racial segregation in schools, parks, restaurants, libraries, movies, churches, and housing. As a consequence, Negro and white children of nursery school age rarely even see one another. White children do have Negro maids in their nursery schools and in their homes, but Negro children seldom have contact with white adults.

Sample

The subjects studied attended six Lynchburg nursery schools, one of which was Negro and the other five white. Two of the white schools were categorized as "lower-status" and three as "upper-status," on the basis of residence and parental occupation of the children attending.† Children in the Negro school came from both lower-status and upper-status families. Some were the

Negro children became aware of race differences at an earlier age than white children. The latter results have been reported by Allport[1] (pp 303, 311) and by Arter[2] (p 186) in a way that implies that Negro children all over the United States become aware of race differences earlier than white.

*In a study of Negro children in Springfield, Massachusetts,[4] (p 175) the Clarks say, in effect, that preference for white means rejection of Negro. Horowitz[6] (p 21) evidently does something similar in equating preference for white with prejudice against Negroes.

†The lower-status schools were day nurseries for mothers who worked in factories, while the upper-status schools were provided for the children of professional people and business executives. Occupations of the parents of lower-status subjects were in the lowest two categories of the "Revised Scale for Rating Occupation,"[18] (pp 140-141) while occupations of parents of upper-status subjects fell into the two top categories. Lower-status children lived in the poorer sections; upper-status children lived in the best residential sections.

children of domestic workers and were subsidized by the Community Fund; others were the children of professional parents who wanted their children to have the opportunities of supervised play. Table 1-I shows the distribution of the 407 subjects as to age, race, and status level. Only those children attending the nursery schools at the time of the study were tested, so there is no claim that the results can be generalized to all children of these ages in Lynchburg.

Data-Collection Technique

The data-collection instrument consisted of a set of pictures of Negroes and whites obtained through professional photographers and pretested over a period of two years. The part of the test reported in this paper concerns the following four pictures: four white children, two boys and two girls, sitting at a table, looking at picture books; four Negro children, two boys and two girls, sitting at a table, looking at picture books; a Negro boy and five white boys and girls at a table, eating; and a white girl and a Negro girl at play, with five Negro boys and girls in the background. The following criteria were utilized in choosing the pictures: the Negro and white children had to be readily identifiable by race, by Negro and white judges; the children had to be of nursery school age and engaged in activity familiar to nursery school children; and the Negro and white children had to be comparable in dress, expression, and activity.* The pictures were in black and white and were eight by ten inches in size.

TABLE 1-I
DISTRIBUTION OF SUBJECTS BY AGE, RACE, AND STATUS LEVEL

Age Category	Negro	Lower White	Upper White
Three	42	42	32
Four	44	62	48
Five	34	40	49
Six	6	3	5
Totals	126	147	134

*This was done to minimize differences in the pictures other than those of race. Selltiz[15] (p 276) points out that measurement of significance based on deviation from random choice implies that the pictures are of equal attractiveness apart from racial characteristics. While the photographs used in this test do not pretend to be identical in all other than racial aspects, such differences were considered unimportant by Negro and white judges.

Interviews were conducted after the interviewer had spent several days becoming acquainted with the children.* The subjects were then invited individually to a separate room "to look at some pictures." Although a few refused to be interviewed or to respond in the interviewing room (none of these are included in the report), the great majority cooperated readily and treated the interview as a picture game. On subsequent days, subjects often asked if they could look at the pictures again.

Measures

Racial acceptance. In order to find out if a child would accept Negro and white children as playmates, he was asked if he would like to play with the children in each of the pictures. A subject was given three chances to say if he would like to play with Negro children, and three chances to say if he would like to play with white children. He was asked to express his willingness to play with groups and with individuals of both sexes. His responses were scored as follows: "acceptance" if he replied a majority of times that he would like to play with the members of the race in question, "nonacceptance" if he replied most frequently that he would not like to play with them for any reason other than racial, and "rejection" if he said most often that he did not want to play with them because of their race.†

Racial preference. Each subject was given three chances to express a preference between Negro and white children in the pictures. He was asked if he would rather play with a group of Negro or white children, with a Negro or a white boy, and with

---

*The author was helped with the interviewing by senior sociology majors, all of whom were trained and supervised by the author. While all of the responses for this paper were obtained by white interviewers, earlier pretesting in which Negro interviewers participated showed no significant differences in the responses by race of the interviewer.

†After each response to the questions of whether he would like to play with the child or children in the pictures, the subject was asked "Why?" or "Why not?" "Nonacceptance" and "rejection" were differentiated by answers to "Why not?" Typical of answers scored as "nonacceptance" were "Jes' cause" or "But I don't even know who they are." Typical answers scored as "rejection" were "I don't like colored people" or "Cause they're black."

a Negro or a white girl. The responses were categorized as "prefer Negro," "prefer white," or "preference not clear," according to the subject's most frequent choice.

RESULTS

Acceptance

Table 1-II summarizes the willingness of the subjects to accept playmates of the other race. Although a significantly greater number of Negro subjects were willing to accept whites than white subjects were to accept Negroes, it is also clear that a sizeable majority of both races accepted members of the other race. Only 3.9 percent of the whites rejected Negroes because of their race, and no Negro rejected a white child on racial grounds.

In order to see if the less frequent acceptance of Negroes by white subjects was a reflection of the whites' greater exclusion of playmates, regardless of race, a comparison was made of the subjects' acceptance of children of their own race. No significant difference in the willingness of Negroes and whites to accept playmates of their own race was found.*

The relationship between the age of the white subjects and their acceptance of Negroes as playmates is summarized in Table 1-III. A significant inverse relationship was obtained, but even at age five more than two-thirds accepted the Negro children in the pictures. As has already been indicated, for a Negro subject of any age not to accept whites was rare.

TABLE 1-II

NEGRO-WHITE DIFFERENCES IN ACCEPTANCE OF PLAYMATES
OF THE OTHER RACE

Response	Negro (N=126) (Percent)	White (N=281) (Percent)
Acceptance of other race	96.8	80.1
Nonacceptance of other race	3.2	16.0
Rejection of other race	0.0	3.9
Chi-square = 19.5 ($p<.001$)		

---

*Of the Negroes, 92.1 percent, and 94.7 percent of the whites accepted playmates of their own race. Chi-square = 1.0 ($p>.30$).

TABLE 1-III

WHITE CHILDREN'S ACCEPTANCE OF NEGRO PLAYMATES
AS RELATED TO AGE*

Response	3-Year-Olds (N=74)	4-Year-Olds (N=110)	5-Year-Olds (N=89)
	(Percent)	*(Percent)*	*(Percent)*
Acceptance of Negroes	90.5	82.7	68.5
Nonacceptance of Negroes	9.5	14.6	22.5
Rejection of Negroes	0.0	2.7	9.0
Chi-square = 12.6 ($p<.01$)			

*The 6-year-olds are not included, since there were too few for statistical significance.

An earlier report on race awareness of Lynchburg nursery school children dealt with variations in the ability of the children to recognize racial differences, or, more specifically, to apply correctly the terms "white" and "colored" to persons in the picture.* In order to see if the ability to recognize racial differences had any relationship to racial acceptance, white subjects of high ability were compared with those of medium and low ability. The difference obtained was not significant (Table 1-IV). Comparing these results with those in Table 1-III, we see that acceptance of

TABLE 1-IV

WHITE CHILDREN'S ACCEPTANCE OF NEGRO PLAYMATES AS
RELATED TO RECOGNITION ABILITY

Response	High Ability (N=179)	Medium and Low Ability (N=102)
	(Percent)	*(Percent)*
Acceptance of Negroes	77.1	85.3
Nonacceptance of Negroes	17.3	13.7
Rejection of Negroes	5.6	1.0
Chi-square = 2.8 ($p>.05$)		

*The part of the test that measured this ability came at the end of the interview. For each of eight pictures, the subject was asked "Do you see a white person in this picture?" If he said he did, he was asked to point to the white person. For the same picture, he was asked "Do you see a colored person in this picture?" If he indicated he did, he was asked to point to the person. Subjects were scored "high" if they were correct on all tries (two for each picture) or if they missed only one, "medium" if they missed two or three, and "low" if they missed four or more.[8] (p 134).

Negroes by whites appears to be more of a function of age than ability to recognize persons as members of a given race.*

The term "prejudice" has not been used to characterize responses of children in this study, but it seems reasonable to consider the lack of willingness to play with a member of another race as a manifestation of prejudice, especially when such refusal is based upon racial considerations. With this in mind, it is of interest to compare the responses of lower-status and upper-status white children, since some studies contend that whites of lower status are more prejudiced against Negroes than those of upper status[9] (pp 597-598),[10] (p 69). Table 1-V compares whites by status level in their acceptance of Negroes as playmates. Since it shows that a significantly greater number of lower-status than upper-status whites accepted Negroes, it does not support the view that there is greater prejudice among lower-status whites, at least for children.†

Preference

Table 1-VI shows that while most of the white subjects preferred to play with children of their own race, a majority of Negro

TABLE 1-V

WHITE CHILDREN'S ACCEPTANCE OF NEGRO PLAYMATES AS
RELATED TO SOCIAL STATUS

	Lower Status (N=147)	Upper Status (N=134)
Response	(Percent)	(Percent)
Acceptance of Negroes	87.8	71.6
Nonacceptance of Negroes	8.8	23.9
Rejection of Negroes	3.4	4.5
Chi-square = 12.3 ($p<.01$)		

*It was likewise found that for Negro subjects, the ability to distinguish between Negroes and whites was not related to their willingness to accept whites as playmates: 97.1 percent of Negroes of high ability accepted whites; 96.7 percent of those of medium and low ability accepted whites.

†It might be asked whether the significantly lower acceptance of Negroes by upper-status white subjects is a reflection, not of unwillingness to play with Negroes as such, but of a more cautious attitude in accepting any child, white or Negro, as a playmate. A comparison of the acceptance of whites by lower-status and upper-status white subjects did reveal that significantly fewer upper-class white subjects were willing to accept the white children in the pictures. Chi-square = 6.7 ($p<.01$).

TABLE 1-VI

NEGRO-WHITE DIFFERENCES IN RACIAL PREFERENCE

Racial Preference	Negro (N=126) (Percent)	White (N=281) (Percent)
Prefer own race	17.5	72.6
Prefer other race	57.9	10.0
Preference not clear	24.6	17.4
Chi-square = 140.4 $(p<.001)$		

subjects preferred to play with children of the other race. Thus, a majority of both Negro and white subjects preferred to play with the white children in the pictures.

This preference for whites was shown by a majority in each age category, in both races (Table 1-VII). While this preference for white over Negro playmates decreases for Negro subjects as age increases, the difference obtained was not significant. However, age was found to be significantly related to the preference scores of white subjects.

Furthermore, according to Table 1-VIII, a majority of subjects of medium and low racial recognition ability, as well as those of high ability, indicated a preference for whites. For both races, the percentages preferring whites were greater for subjects of high ability. The difference obtained was significant for white but not for Negro subjects.

A final inquiry about racial preference concerns its relationship to the status level of white subjects. Table 1-IX reveals that

TABLE 1-VII

AGE AND NEGRO-WHITE DIFFERENCES IN RACIAL PREFERENCE*

	Negroes			Whites		
	3 Years (N=42)	4 Years (N=44)	5 Years (N=34)	3 Years (N=74)	4 Years (N=110)	5 Years (N=89)
Racial Preference	(Percent)	(Percent)	(Percent)	(Percent)	(Percent)	(Percent)
Prefer Negro	11.9	25.0	14.7	10.8	10.9	7.9
Prefer white	64.3	59.1	50.0	59.5	78.2	75.3
Preference not clear	23.8	15.9	35.3	29.7	10.9	16.9
Chi-square for Negroes = 5.9 $(p>.20)$						
Chi-square for whites = 11.6 $(p<.05)$						

*The 6-year-olds are not included, since there were too few for statistical significance.

TABLE 1-VIII

RACIAL PREFERENCE AS RELATED TO RACE AND
RACIAL RECOGNITION ABILITY

	Negroes		Whites	
	High Ability (N=35)	*Medium and Low Ability (N=91)*	*High Ability (N=179)*	*Medium and Low Ability (N=102)*
Racial Preference	*(Percent)*	*(Percent)*	*(Percent)*	*(Percent)*
Prefer Negro	17.1	17.6	8.4	12.7
Prefer white	65.7	54.9	78.2	62.7
Preference not clear	17.1	27.5	13.4	24.5

Chi-square for Negroes = 1.6 $(p>.30)$
Chi-square for white = 8.1 $(p<.02)$

a significantly larger percentage of lower-status than upper-status whites expressed a preference for whites. A significantly greater preference for whites by lower-status white subjects was found when whites of high racial recognition ability were compared; however, no significant difference by status was found between white subjects of medium and low recognition ability.*

CONCLUSIONS

Several findings emerge from this study:

1. A large majority of the subjects of both races "accepted" both Negro and white playmates, with very few rejecting them for racial reasons.† Since acceptance of children of the other race was the rule and rejection rare, it can be concluded that little

TABLE 1-IX

WHITE CHILDREN'S RACIAL PREFERENCE AS
RELATED TO SOCIAL STATUS

Racial Preference	*Lower-Status (N=147) (Percent)*	*Upper Status (N=134) (Percent)*
Prefer Negro	4.8	15.7
Prefer white	81.6	62.7
Preference not clear	13.6	21.6

Chi-square = 10.8 $(p<.01)$

---

*For those of high ability, chi-square = 10.857 $(p<.01)$. For those of medium and low ability, chi-square = 5.0 $(p>.05)$.

†It will be recalled, however, from Table 1-II, that a significantly larger number of Negro subjects accepted whites than white subjects accepted Negroes.

racial prejudice was shown by the subjects. These results question whether a racially segregated environment in itself brings about prejudice in the child by the time he is of nursery school age.*

2. Both Negro and white subjects were more likely to "prefer" the white to the Negro children in the pictures. It may be hypothesized, then, that children reared in a racially segregated environment will develop a bias for whites at an early age, unless they encounter parental or other instruction counteracting the impact of environmental influence.† Such an hypothesis could be tested by studying children who deviate from the majority in racial attitudes. However, a similar preference for whites has been reported in studies of children in northern, nonsegregated nursery schools.‡ Perhaps then, the racial preference of our southern subjects reflects, at least in part, a reaction to the less favorable position of the Negro in American society as a whole.

3. Preference for one race did not imply rejection of the other. When no choice between Negro and white playmates was asked for, the subjects readily accepted Negro children. *It might be said, then, that the majority of subjects manifested racial bias, but not necessarily racial prejudice.*§

4. A significantly larger number of white subjects of lower than of upper status accepted Negroes as playmates, but, on the other hand, proportionately more lower-status than upper-status

---

*Although the following two named studies used measurement instruments different from those used in this study and different from one another, they support this doubt as to whether a segregated system in itself develops race prejudice in young children. Horowitz[6] (pp 21-22) found no significant difference in the prejudice of children from New York City and those from Georgia and Tennessee. The Clarks[4] (p 175) found no significant difference in the prejudice of Negro children in Massachusetts and those in Arkansas.

†Clark,[3] (pp 25-36) however, raises questions about the effectiveness of teaching by parents, church, and schools that runs counter to the impact of the social setting, in which the Negro is at a disadvantage economically and socially, and in which he is either ignored or portrayed unfavorably in mass media.

‡For example, with Negro nursery school children in Springfield, Massachusetts,[4] (p 175) with Negro and white nursery school children in a New England city,[5] (p 63) with Negro and white elementary school children in New York City,[6] (pp 21-22) and with Negro and white children in kindergarten through the second grade in Philadelphia.[17] (p 141).

§The author follows the distinction between "prejudice" and "bias" suggested by Schermerhorn[14] (pp 482-483).

white subjects expressed a preference for white playmates. In other words, the lower-status white subjects showed a stronger preference for whites than did the upper-status white subjects, while at the same time they showed greater willingness to accept Negroes. These results appear to be contradictory, but they are in accord with another conclusion of this study, namely, that preferring the members of one race does not necessarily mean that members of the other race will be unacceptable, when no choice has to be made.

5. A preference for whites was shown by a majority of subjects, including the youngest and those of medium and low racial recognition ability. This indicates that preference for whites by children of both races developed early, even before racial differences could be communicated. Such results can be interpreted to mean that learning to prefer whites comes through "indirect" rather than through "direct" verbal instruction.* Furthermore, these results underline a conclusion reached by a number of investigators, namely, that racial attitudes are derived indirectly, rather than from direct contact with members of the race itself.[11,13] In the Lynchburg setting, strict racial segregation makes direct contact between Negro and white children rare. Yet, at nursery school age both have learned to prefer white playmates.

REFERENCES

1. ALLPORT, GORDON: *The Nature of Prejudice.* Cambridge, Mass., Addison-Wesley, 1954.
2. ARTER, RHETTA M.: The effects of prejudice on children. *Children,* 6:185-189, 1959.
3. CLARK, K. B.: *Prejudice and Your Child.* Boston, Beacon, 1955.
4. CLARK, K.B., and CLARK, M. P.: Racial identification and preference in Negro children. In T. M. Newcomb and E. L. Hartley (Eds.): *Readings in Social Psychology.* New York, Holt, 1947, pp. 169-178.
5. GOODMAN, M. E.: *Race Awareness in Young Children.* Cambridge, Mass., Addison Wesley, 1952.

---

*Quinn[11] (p 42) in a study of the transmission of racial attitudes in white Southerners reports, "Where racial attitudes are concerned, direct verbal instruction seems to play a relatively unimportant part. . . For the most part, verbal instruction is avoided; even when it is given, it is usually justified in other than racial terms."

6. HOROWITZ, E. L.: The development of attitude toward the Negro. *Arch. Psychol.*, (194), 1936.
7. HOROWITZ, RUTH: Racial aspects of self-identification in nursery school children. *J. Psychol.*, 7:91-99, 1939.
8. MORLAND, J. K.: Racial recognition by nursery school children in Lynchburg, Virginia. *Social forces*, 37:132-137, 1958.
9. MYRDAL, GUNNAR: *An American Dilemna.* New York, Harpers, 1944.
10. POPE, LISTON: *Millhands and Preachers.* New Haven, Yale, 1942.
11. QUINN, OLIVE: The transmission of racial attitudes among white southerners. *Social Forces*, 33:41-47, 1954.
12. RADKE, MARIAN, and TRAGER, HELEN: Children's perception of the social roles of Negroes and whites. *J. Psychol.*, 29:3-33, 1950.
13. REINMANN, MIRIAM: How children become prejudiced. In M. L. Barron (Ed.): *American Minorities.* New York, Knopf, 1957, pp. 94-104.
14. SCHERMERHORN, R. A.: *These Our People.* Boston, Heath, 1949.
15. SELLTIZ, CLAIRE, et al.: *Research Methods in Social Relations.* (Revised). New York, Holt, 1959.
16. SPRINGER, DORIS: Awareness of racial differences by pre-school children in Hawaii, *Genet. Psychol. Monogr.*, 41:215-270, 1950.
17. TRAGER, H. G., and YARROW, M. R.: *They Learn What They Live.* New York, Harpers, 1952.
18. WARNER, W. L., et al.: *Social Class in America.* Chicago, Sci. Res. Assoc., 1949.

Chapter 2

CONCEPT FORMATION AND THE DEVELOPMENT OF ETHNIC AWARENESS

GRAHAM M. VAUGHAN

Victoria University of Wellington
Wellington, New Zealand

The term "concept" has been defined by Heidbreder[4] (p 3) as "a logical construct which, by means of symbols or signs, may be used interpersonally," and "concept formation" by Kendler[7] (p 447) as "the acquisition or utilization, or both, of a common response to dissimilar stimuli." Considered in this light, it follows that a concept provides for the organism one tool whereby some degree of mastery over the environment can be achieved; and the attainment of a concept is congruent with the extent to which the organism has differentiated and structured its environment.

How do concepts originate? Logically, it could be argued that, before a common response to dissimilar stimuli can be achieved, the organism must first be able to discriminate between the stimuli in question. In discussing this point, Bruner, Goodnow, and Austin[1] (p 1) wrote: ". . . to categorize is to render discriminably different things equivalent, to group the objects and events and people around us into classes, and to respond to them in terms of their class membership rather than their uniqueness." Learning to categorize, the authors continue, provides a principal means by which socialization proceeds, and concept attainment reflects, to some extent, the demands of one's culture.

Note. Reprinted by permission from *The Journal of Genetic Psychology, 103*:93-103, 1963. This research was supported by funds granted by the Carnegie Corporation of New York to Victoria University of Wellington. The author wishes to thank Dr. G. L. Mangan for his helpful criticisms of the manuscript, although the author must accept full responsibility for views expressed.

A complication arises when a "discriminations-leading-to-cate-
gorization" analysis, as outlined above, is applied to the problem
of the development of ethnic awareness in young children. For
in this instance, the child is discriminating between, and eventually categorizing, people rather than things. A distinction is
drawn here between thing-objects and person-objects. Where the
latter are involved, the organism is faced with a situation in which
it has attributes in common with one or more discriminable stimuli. Using an oddity problem to illustrate, suppose that a young
white S is asked to choose the odd one from among one white and
two colored people. A failure of S to make the correct choice
could be interpreted in two ways: (a) he is incapable of discriminating between the colors involved (which is unlikely); or (b) the
color discrimination is not considered by S to be a factor of importance, and the stimuli are rendered equivalent in that they are
all people. At any rate, in concluding on this evidence that S is
completely incapable of discriminating ethnic differences, one
could be turning a blind eye to certain restrictions imposed by
the oddity task method. At this point, an alternative theoretical
proposition is offered: according to the extent of differentiation
between self and environment, it is conceivable that a young S
will revert to a primitive discriminative mechanism of "identification" where other means of discrimination are ineffective.

In treating the problem of identification, Freud[2,3] referred to
an undifferentiated perception of an external object and the self
in the initial states of development (primary identification), which
gives way in later development to a discrimination of a world of
objects separate from the self, including some with which the
organism may identify (secondary identification). More recently,
Kagan[6] analyzed the term identification within a learning theory
framework, proposing that the main goal states of identification
are (a) mastery of the environment and (b) love and affection,
in contradistinction to Freud's view that identification provides
a means for reducing anxiety arising from oedipal conflict. For
the purposes of the present report, attention is directed to Kagan's
proposition that mastery of the environment can be associated with
the process of identification. The implication for a study of ethnic
awareness is that it should be possible to organize within the one

schema the processes of identification, self-differentiation, discrimination, and concept attainment.

PROBLEM

In view of the points considered above, it would be reasonable to predict that ethnic awareness will depend initially upon the perception of discriminably different objects. However, since a concept of race is derived from categorizing attributes of person-objects rather than thing-objects, it is likely that an identification process may also be involved. In the present study, it was hypothesized that the ontogenetic appearance of the phenomena relating to the formation of an ethnic concept would be as follows:

1. Identification by race with person-objects.
2. Discrimination by race between person-objects.
3. Attainment of a concept of race.

The problem of distinguishing between these three proposed "levels of awarenesss" was felt to be largely a methodological one. In this respect, Johnson's discussion[5] of the traditional methods for investigating concept formation provides a useful theoretical setting. Two basic methods are outlined: (a) free response and (b) objective discrimination. Usually, the former is more appropriate for testing the personal meaning of a concept, and the latter for the standardized (cultural) meaning. It has also been found that these methods differ with respect to the criteria of task mastery involved, in that some *S*s can pass some tests but not others. Johnson[5] (p 233) concludes that "as in any other area of science, the results are determined in part by the method, and the best results come from a convergence of two or more methods."

The construction of a test continuum based on task difficulty, incorporating both the free response and objective discrimination methods, was considered to be a worthwhile approach to testing the adequacy of the three awareness levels proposed in this study. An awareness level is here defined as "task mastery at a specified point on the test continuum." The nature of the test continuum constructed for this research is discussed more fully following the description of the test material.

METHOD
Subjects

The Ss were 180 white children enrolled in four nursery and primary schools in Wellington, New Zealand, a city with a population of 237,000 whites and 3,500 Maoris in the year 1960. The children ranged in chronological age (CA) from four through 12 years, 20 Ss being assigned to each of nine CA groups at successive one-year intervals. The group means by age (years and months) were as follows: 4.0, 5.4, 6.0, 7.1, 8.1, 9.0, 10.2, 11.0, and 12.1. All groups were divided evenly according to sex. A few Maoris attended each of the nurseries and schools, so that some play contact between the two races was possible. The Ss were selected at random from class rolls.

Materials

Seven tests employing doll and picture materials were constructed for this study. The purpose of the tests was to investigate stages in the development of the concept "Maori." The tests were as follows: picture identification, doll identification, picture discrimination, doll discrimination, doll assembly, doll classification (part A), and doll classification (part B). The picture materials were constructed from a set used in a previous study.[10]

1. *Picture identification.* Six picture sketches showing three whites and three Maoris, all of the same sex as S, were arranged, in random fashion before S who was asked "Which child looks most like you?" A response was recorded in terms of whether a white or Maori figure was chosen.

2. *Doll identification.* Two two-dimensional hardboard dolls seven inches high of the same sex as S were used. One doll was painted to represent a white and the other a Maori. Each S was shown the dolls and asked "Which doll looks most like you?" A response was recorded in terms of whether a white or Maori doll was chosen.

3. *Picture discrimination.* Similar in design to a test used by Stevenson and Stewart,[9] this test consisted of 18 six by four inch pictures, 12 (six male, six female) of which were related to race while the remaining six were employed as fillers. Each S received

the fillers, followed by six race cards depicting figures of the same sex as S. The pictures were presented to S in four sets, three pictures at a time. The two filler sets (showing two aeroplanes and a yacht, two apples and a banana) were shown in turn to the S, who was asked to indicate the picture that differed from the other two. At this stage, a correctional procedure was adopted when S made an incorrect response. Following this, the two race sets (showing one white and two Maoris, two whites and one Maori, all of same sex as S) were presented together with the same instruction, but without corrections being offered by E. A response was recorded as correct if the figure differing by race was chosen. All sets were presented so that the correct choice varied through three horizontal positions: left, middle, and right.

4. *Doll discrimination.* Three female dolls 12 inches high, made of a flesh-colored vinyl, were used. The dolls were dressed in green frocks, white bonnets, and white boots, and were identical in appearance except that two had pink skin and blue eyes (white dolls), while the other had brown skin and brown eyes (Maori doll). A response was recorded as correct if the Maori doll was chosen as being different.

5. *Doll assembly.* Two two-dimensional dolls seven inches high, of the same sex as S, were used. Each doll consisted of six pieces: a head, a torso, two arms, and two legs. One set of pieces was painted pink and the other brown. The S's task was to assemble the 12 pieces, presented in random array, so as to make two dolls. A response was recorded as all correct if S assembled the dolls without mixing the pieces by color.

6. *Doll classification (part A).* A brown-skinned doll similar in make to those dolls used in the doll discrimination test was used. This doll, however, was dressed in traditional Maori costume: a grass skirt, a feathered cape, a *tiki,** and a headband. S was asked "What sort of doll is this?" A response was recorded as correct if the word "Maori" was used.

7. *Doll classification (part B).* At the conclusion of the doll discrimination test, and prior to part A of the doll classification test, E pointed to the brown-skinned doll dressed in a white's

---

*A traditional Maori amulet.

clothing and casually enquired of S "What sort of doll is this?"
As in part A above, a response was recorded as correct if the word
"Maori" was used.

Relation Between Materials and Test Continuum

The seven tests used are discussed below in relation to the three
proposed awareness levels.

Identification tests. Tests 1 and 2 require S to identify by physical appearance a picture with a doll. Since the tests are structured,
and as S's response can be nonverbal, they could be placed in the
objective method category. The main psychological factor presumed to be operating is idenification, associated with a low-level
discrimination, (differentiation of self from the dissimilar figure).
These tests, then, were designed to measure *low* awareness.

Discrimination tests. Tests 3 and 4 consist of two oddity tasks
using picture and doll materials. Once again, these tests are included in the objective method category for the same reasons
noted above. The discriminative process in this case, however,
requires something more than identification on the part of S, i.e.
the tests were designed to measure *medium* awareness.

Assembly test. The test instruction "Make up two dolls out
of these pieces" implies "Put those things together that belong
together." The task, therefore, requires S to categorize as well as
to discriminate. Johnson[5] has referred to a test of this kind as a
limited free response method. In terms of the test continuum used
in the present study, the doll assembly test was designed to provide
a task whose difficulty was intermediate between the discrimination tests and the classification tests. Since a verbal response is
not essential to mastery, success per se in this test does not indicate
concept attainment. Its purpose, therefore, was to measure the
upper limit of medium awareness.

Classification tests. Both of these tests employ the question
"What sort of a doll is this?" and could be included in the free
response category. S's task is now verbal, and the accuracy of his
description provides a measure of not only task mastery, but also
mastery of the concept "Maori." When the brown-skinned doll was
dressed in traditional Maori costume (part A), it was assumed

that cues pointing to the correct verbal response were maximal, while the substitution of a white's clothing (part B) was a restriction upon the cues available. These two tests, then, in the order given above, were designed to approach the end point in the envisaged test continuum, and served to measure concept attainment or *high* awareness.

Procedure

The general order of presentation was to show *S* the picture material initally, then the two-dimensional dolls, and finally the three-dimensional dolls. The tests were imbedded within a larger battery relating to ethnic attitudes, the results of which will be reported at a future date. *S*s were tested individually at school. Testing time per *S* averaged about 15 minutes.

RESULTS

The focus of attention in this study was directed towards a comparison between a number of age groups in terms of correct responses to seven ethnic awareness tests. The proportion of *S*s at each CA from four through 12 making correct responses on each of the seven tests is shown in Table 2-I. An indication is given in the table where statistical tests are not applicable (n.a.).

A preliminary analysis of the data shown in Table 2-I revealed that the general tendency for all *S*s ($N = 180$) was to make significantly more correct than incorrect responses to each of the seven tests. The means of the proportions for the tests ranged between .61 and .92, and the attached correct response (CR) values satisfied a test of significance at the .01 level. The proportion of correct responses was found to be positively correlated with age ($p < .01$) for tests 3, 5, 6, and 7. Correlations based on CA group rankings were not applicable for tests 1, 2, and 4, in that the tendency for correct responses to increase with age leveled off at early CA levels. However, the overall trend was the same: for each test, the proportion of correct responses increased with age until a stable level of performance was reached.

A secondary analysis of these data was carried out to determine the earliest CA for each test at which a significant proportion of *S*s made correct responses. The results of this analysis are incorporated in Table 2-I in the form of asterisks indicating the earliest age at which mastery of each task was achieved. An inspection of these results reveals a general tendency for identification tests to be mastered before discrimination tests, and for the latter to be mastered before classification tests, in terms of age. As it was not clear before testing whether task difficulty was related to the nature of the materials used (in the present case, dolls and pictures), the ordering of test 1 in relation to 2 and of 3 in relation to 4 along the y-axis is a post hoc one which maximizes the predicted trend.

No consistent or significant sex differences were found in any aspect of the present research.

DISCUSSION

The discussion of results presented below is restricted to the secondary analysis of the relation between CA and task mastery on each of the seven tests, and the implication of this analysis for the treatment of the development of ethnic awareness within a concept-formation framework.

In general, the research hypothesis was supported. The simplest tests (tests 1 and 2), tapping a low-level form of ethnic awareness, involved identification.

The instruction "Show me the one like you" is one that has clear meaning for four-year-old Ss who mastered one of the two tests. The concept of self would appear to be operative in young Ss to the extent that they are capable of nominating their membership to a group similar in race to themselves.

The discrimination tests, based on oddity problems (tests 3 and 4), presented tasks which were somewhat more difficult. One was mastered at CA five, and both at CA six. Mastery at this point indicates that S has progressed beyond identifying with his ethnic group to the extent that he can distinguish between other members of the ingroup on one hand, and members of an outgroup on the other. This mastery has been defined above as medium awareness.*

---

*An anomaly in the results relating to identification tests was that task mastery was achieved at an earlier CA when picture rather than doll material is considered. The results for the discrimination tests, however, provide a reversed trend. One possible explanation is that, while color is a more immediate cue in an oddity problem than is a combination of facial features and achromatic shading, the subtler nature of the latter ones assumes importance in a task involving self-identification.

TABLE 2-I

PROPORTION OF 20 CHILDREN AT EACH OF NINE AGE LEVELS MAKING CORRECT
RESPONSES ON SEVEN AWARENESS TESTS

Test[a]	Age Level									Mean	CR	Rho
	4	5	6	7	8	9	10	11	12			
1. Picture identification	.75*	.80	1.00	1.00	.90	1.00	.90	.95	.95	.92	11.80	n.a.
2. Doll identification	.60	.85*	.85	.80	.80	.95	.90	.90	.80	.83	8.80	n.a.
3. Picture discrimination	.53	.55	.68[b]*	.70	.70	.70	.73	.83	.73	.68[c]	n.a.	.954
4. Doll discrimination	.70	.75*	.95	1.00	.95	.95	.95	.95	.95	.91	10.73	n.a.
5. Doll assembly	.20	.55	.60	.85*	1.00	1.00	1.00	1.00	1.00	.79	7.90	1.00
6. Doll classification (A)	.55	.60	.55	.80*	.70	1.00	.95	1.00	1.00	.82	8.64	.925
7. Doll classification (B)	.35	.30	.40	.65	.70	.70	.75*	.80	.80	.61	2.83	.975

[a] The data at each CA for tests 1, 2, 3, 4, 5, 6, and 7 were tested for significance by the sign test, and that for test 3 by the chi-square test. Both tests 3 and 4 were oddity tasks involving three objects at a time, the probability of a correct choice being 1:3. However, since this study is concerned with the extent to which each CA group has *mastered* each task, the data for tests 3 and 4 were tested for significance against a chance probability of 1:2 rather than 1:3.

[b] Based on data derived from two sets of three pictures ($x^2 = 6.10$, $df = 2$, $p < .05$).

[c] $x^2 = 47.69$, $df = 2$, $p < .001$.

* Significant at the .05 level.

Mastery of the doll assembly test was achieved at CA seven, one year later than the CA related to the discrimination tests, indicating that, in terms of awareness levels, the test does fall at the predicted point on the test continuum—intermediate between the discrimination and classification tests. Because the verbal response "Maori" is not essential to mastery, however, this test is appropriately located at a point between medium and high awareness.

Mastery of the doll classification test (part A) was also achieved at CA seven, indicating that this age represents a transitional point at which the degree of ethnic awareness is associated with a somewhat restricted concept of race. Using the present battery of tests, no improvement in task mastery was noted at CA eight or nine, indicating that the concept "Maori" is limited in meaning to figures clothed in traditional Maori costume. It is not until CA ten that full mastery of both parts A and B of this test is achieved. At this age, Ss were successful in mastering all tests offered, and were not dependent on the cue of traditional costume to make the verbal response "Maori." On the present test continuum, no further improvement was allowed for, so it appeared that a well-developed concept of race had been attained at ten years of age. It is possible that the use of a more refined test continuum, e.g., one including a picture classification test, might eliminate the plateaux in awareness development noted at CA seven to nine and CA ten to twelve.

It was concluded that the attainment of a concept of race is dependent upon a capacity to render discriminably different stimuli equivalent. Since the concept involves person-objects rather than thing-objects, however, an identification response precedes ontogenetically the more usual discrimination response.

A final point is worth noting. The problem of the development of ethnic awareness has been here treated within a concept-formation framework. If an effective component is incorporated within this treatment, the scope of theory can be extended to the problem of attitude development. Rhine[8] has already contemplated this possibility.

SUMMARY

In this study, the nature of the development of ethnic awareness is examined within a framework of concept formation. The view that a capacity to render discriminably different stimuli equivalent is a prerequisite to concept attainment is probably sufficient where concrete objects are involved. It was hypothesized that in the case of the development of ethnic awareness, however, the discriminative process underlying the attainment of a concept of race includes a process of identification on S's part with one or more of the perceived objects. Seven tests of ethnic awareness, designed to measure low-level (identification tests), medium-level (discrimination tests), and high-level awareness (classification tests), were administered to 180 Ss in the age range four to twelve years. The research hypothesis was supported, and it was concluded that where the concept of race is involved, an identification response precedes ontogenetically the more usual discrimination response. By incorporating an affective component, the theoretical scope of the treatment of awareness development within a concept-formation framework can be extended to the problem of attitude development.

REFERENCES

1. BRUNER, J. S., GOODNOW, J. J., and AUSTIN, G. A.: *A Study of Thinking.* New York, Wiley, 1956.
2. FREUD, S.: *New Introductory Lectures on Psychoanalysis.* New York, Norton, 1933.
3. FREUD, S.: *The Ego and the Id.* London, Hogarth, 1935.
4. HEIDBREDER, E.: Toward a dynamic psychology of cognition. *Psychol. Rev., 52*:1-22, 1945.
5. JOHNSON, D. M.: *The Psychology of Thought and Judgment.* New York, Harper, 1955.
6. KAGAN, J.: The concept of identification. *Psychol. Rev., 65*:296-305, 1958.
7. KENDLER, T. S.: Concept formation. *Ann. Rev. Psychol., 12*:447-472, 1961.
8. RHINE, R. J.: A concept-formation approach to attitude acquisition. *Psychol. Rev., 65*:364-369, 1958.
9. STEVENSON, H. W., and STEWART, E. C.: A developmental study of racial awareness in young children. *Child Devel. 29*:399-409, 1958.
10. VAUGHAN, G. M., and THOMPSON, R. H. T.: New Zealand children's attitudes towards Maoris. *J. Abnorm. Soc. Psychol., 62*: 701-704, 1961.

Chapter 3

A COMPARISON OF CERTAIN ATTITUDINAL RESPONSES OF WHITE AND NEGRO HIGH SCHOOL STUDENTS

PAUL L. BOYNTON and GEORGE DOUGLAS MAYO

The problem under analysis is not an altogether new one, nor are the techniques employed used without precedent. The study does differ from certain others in the field, however, in that it takes what might be called the rural or small town high school students in both racial groups, and studies their reactions to a group of problems known to be or to have been matters of some concern in the general section of the country in which the study was made. Nevertheless, the authors readily acknowledge an indebtedness both as to content and form to previous investigators such as Bryant,[1] Davis,[2] Bolton,[3] Katz and Braly,[4] and Smith.[5]

The matter of the meaning of the term "attitude" is always a problem with a questionable solution. In this study it is defined merely in terms of the responses which the students made to the test which was given them. In the present discussion the term "attitude" is used almost synonymously with "opinion," though the authors themselves recognize a difference in the terms.

The test employed cannot claim to be exhaustive. In fact, attitudinal influences are so subtle that they frequently are not recognized. Hence almost any test may be a test of attitude. So no attempt was made to cover all fields of Negro-white relations. At the same time, an attempt, of a purely subjective nature, to be sure, was made to sample a fairly wide range of problems associated with the interrelated activities of the two races. The 24 items which finally were used in the test are the residual items from a

Note: Reprinted by permission from *The Journal of Negro Education*, 11:487-494, 1942.

much larger list which was prepared originally. Careful study and criticism of the original list finally resulted in the elimination of all items but these 24. It must be recognized, though, that the final selection of items was arbitrary. The test, together with the directions, was given as indicated below:

Before you start the test indicate your grade in school, your age, and whether you are a boy or a girl in the blanks provided. You will not sign your name; so feel free to respond to each part of the test with complete frankness. On this test there are no right or wrong answers; just score the items according to what you think about the matter proposed. You will notice under each item the terms *True, Probably True, Don't Know, Probably False,* and *False.* If you are sure you agree with the statement, draw a line under the word TRUE. If you think you agree with the statement but are not sure, underscore the term PROBABLY TRUE. If you do not have any very definite opinion on the matter one way or the other, or don't know anything about it, underscore the term DON'T KNOW. If you think you disagree with the statement but are not sure, underscore the term PROB-ABLY FALSE. If you are sure you disagree with the statement, underscore the word FALSE. You will have plenty of time; so read every item very carefully and answer frankly. Remember, you are not to sign your name.

Grade_____   Age_____   Sex_____

1. The Negro and the white man have about the same natural ability.

2. A Negro has a right to a fair trial in court regardless of what he has done.

3. It is all right for a Negro to sit on the same seat of an automobile with a white man.

4. Negroes should be allowed to vote in all elections, including Democratic primaries.

5. Most Negroes should be satisfied with being servants.

6. A white man should never strike a Negro if he would not hit a white man under the same conditions.

7. Negro children should be allowed to attend the same school that white children attend.

8. A white man should shake hands with a Negro without hesitation.

9. It is all right for whites and Negroes to work together on P.W.A. projects, in the field, or in other such forms of work.

10. All Negroes should be forced to leave the United States.

11. If a Negro driving a car gets to a one-way bridge slightly

before a car driven by a white man arrives at the other end, it is all right for the Negro to make the white man wait.

12. The average Negro is physically superior to the average white man.

13. The inability of the Negroes to develop outstanding leaders dooms them to a low place in society.

14. The educated Negro is less of a burden on the courts and is less likely to become a dependent or a defective than the educated white man.

15. Negroes should be allowed to sit with white people in the movies.

16. If two white men, walking together on a walk that is only wide enough for two, meet a Negro, one of the white men should drop behind the other to let the Negro pass.

17. All Negroes should answer all grown white men by saying, "Yes, sir," or "No, sir," rather than "Yes," or "No."

18. White filling station attendants should wipe the windshield and check the tires and water for Negro automobile owners.

19. There should not be a law forbidding the marriage of whites and Negroes.

20. Negroes should be allowed to eat ice cream at a table in a drug store the same as whites.

21. Negroes who can afford to buy Pullman car tickets should be permitted to do so when traveling long distances on a train.

22. The Negro should be given the same social advantages as the white man.

23. Negroes should not be permitted to live near the homes of white people, unless they live in servants' houses.

24. Negro barbers should be allowed to cut the hair of both whites and Negroes.

The study involves 177 Negro boys, 290 Negro girls, 199 white boys, and 261 white girls. All were high school students at the time the responses were made. The Negroes are all the Negroes who were present at the time of testing in four Negro high schools of three western Tennessee counties, with the exception of a few who did not answer all the items. These were rural senior high schools, and, jointly, enrolled most of the Negroes in high school in the counties in which they were located. Two of the same three counties supplied the white students. These latter were located in three senior high schools, which cared for most of the white children in high school in the counties.

No attempt was made to investigate and hold constant for the two groups such factors as socioeconomic status, scholastic aptitude, intelligence, or emotionality. The investigation was more a status study, a study of what is, than a study of causes.

In Table 3-I will be found a summary, in terms of percentages, of the popularity of each type of response to each item for all students of both races, along with an indication of those percentage differences which are statistically reliable, or are as much as 3.83 times their respective probable errors. Here we note that on only two of the items, 2 and 19, did there fail to be a statistically significant percentage difference in *both* of the extreme positions. Item 2 indicates that a Negro has a right to a fair trial in court regardless of what he has done. This is accepted as true by a majority of both races, but 27 percent more Negroes accept it completely than do whites. Probably more interesting than the percentages of acceptance are the percentages of rejection or probable rejection of the principle. Here we find that 9 percent of whites and 8 percent of Negroes are in general disagreement with the idea of the Negro always having what might be called legal justice. While it is probably alarming that about one white out of ten did not concede this legal equality to the Negro, it would seem to be absolutely startling to note that about one Negro out of ten is prone to accept as justifiable a curtailment of his full rights of a "fair trial."

Item number 19 relates to the desirability of laws prohibiting interracial marriage. It is interesting to note that about one out of every four students of both races definitely disfavor this legal prohibition of biracial marriage. True, a significantly larger percent of white than of Negro children favored this restriction, but, even so, about one Negro out of every two thought the legal restriction to be desirable. Of course, this probably points to the fact that the average of these Negro students was definitely interested in racial purity or racial autonomy, as was the case, though somewhat more strongly, with the white group.

If we concern ourselves with the items which showed the greatest disagreement in opinion between the races, we might note especially items 20, 8, 22, 4, 16, 15, and 17. These have been selected by the following procedure: first, compute the amount of difference in the combined "True" and "Probably True" judg-

Prejudice in Children

TABLE 3-I

Percentages of All White and All Negro Students, Both Sexes, Who Responded in Each of Five Possible Ways to Each of the 24 Test Items, Together with Indications of All Percentage Differences, for Any Response Level, Which Are Statistically Reliable

		Percentages					Statistically Reliable Differences				
Item	Race	True	Prob. True	Don't Know	Prob. False	False	True	Don't Know	Prob. False	Prob. True	False
1	W	10	26	7	13	43	*		W	W	W
	N	52	26	2	3	17	N				
2	W	57	11	2	3	6		W			
	N	84	6	2	3	5	N				
3	W	20	21	6	13	40				W	W
	N	56	19	5	6	14	N				
4	W	22	14	11	10	43			W	W	W
	N	75	14	5	2	3	N				
5	W	33	23	11	13	20	W	W			
	N	10	9	8	11	61					N
6	W	44	18	7	10	21		W	W	W	W
	N	86	6	2	3	3	N				
7	W	1	1	—	2	96					W
	N	21	18	6	9	46	N	N	N	N	
8	W	2	5	5	10	78					W
	N	55	19	8	7	10	N	N			
9	W	30	31	10	12	18		W	W	W	W
	N	69	18	3	3	7	N				
10	W	9	7	11	12	62	W	W	W	W	
	N	1	1	5	5	88					N
11	W	28	19	8	10	35			W	W	W
	N	69	15	4	5	7	N				
12	W	18	20	26	9	27					W
	N	36	22	27	6	8	N				
13	W	30	2	28	10	10	W				
	N	15	16	25	13	31		N	N		N
14	W	17	15	25	15	29				W	W
	N	25	22	23	9	21	N	N	N		
15	W	—	—	1	4	94					W
	N	29	15	5	10	41	N	N	N	N	
16	W	29	17	5	8	41		W		W	W
	N	88	5	3	1	3	N				
17	W	86	9	1	2	2	W				
	N	34	14	4	7	41			N	N	N
18	W	45	22	11	8	15		W	W	W	W
	N	83	9	3	2	4	N				
19	W	23	3	3	3	68					W
	N	24	8	13	4	49		N	N		

TABLE 3-I—*Continued*

		Percentages					Statistically Reliable Differences				
Item	*Race*	*True*	*Prob. True*	*Don't Know*	*Prob. False*	*False*	*True*	*Don't Know*	*Prob. False*	*Prob. True*	*False*
20	W	2	4	3	7	85					W
	N	63	18	3	6	10	N	N	N		
21	W	8	16	29	2	34			W	W	W
	N	58	18	18	3	3	N				
22	W	8	13	12	4	53			W	W	W
	N	82	11	3	1	3	N				
23	W	39	20	8	7	16	W	W		W	
	N	11	11	5	10	63					N
24	W	7	10	5	9	70					W
	N	38	17	7	8	30	N	N	N		

* An N indicates that the percent of Negroes who answered an item in a designated manner is reliably greater, statistically, than the percent of whites who answered the same item in the same manner. A W indicates that a statistically reliably larger number of whites than Negroes made the particular answer to the question or item under consideration.

ments, and the amount of difference in the combined "False" and "Probably False" judgments, and add the differences for a total percent of difference. This procedure resulted in the selection and order of items just listed.

To some it may seem strange that the item which showed the greatest disagreement is a relatively trivial matter, that of Negroes eating ice cream in a drug store. (Drug stores in this section are run by white persons.) In reality it probably is merely indicative of the fact that there is more disagreement between the races with respect to the problem of "social equality" than there is with respect to matters involving political, legal, or economic equality. This conclusion is made even more evident when we combine the findings on item 20 with those of items 22 and 8. These three are the items about which there is definitely the most pronounced and unequivocal difference. Item 22 involves giving the Negro social advantages comparable to that of the white, and item 8 involves a white man shaking hands with a Negro. It would seem that in all three instances the main question facing the white students was merely that of whether they should admit some doubt about the desirability of sharp social inequality, and, with the Negro, whether to admit a doubt as to the desirability of definite social equality. In fact, among these seven items which show the most total difference in opinion, only number 4, that of voting in the "White Man's Primary," does not relate itself almost wholly to the matter of social barriers between the races. Although there are differences in opinion with respect to the other problems, the main line of cleavage between the races was definitely with respect to the matter of social distinction, and, rather strikingly, is exhibited with respect to items which when looked at in a detached manner actually are of little consequence one way or the other.

When attention is turned to the items about which there is the least disagreement, we note 2, 19, 13, 14, 12, and 18. The first of these pertains to legal equality, and the next to both legal equality and racial autonomy, the third to education or probably to basic ability, the fourth to education, the fifth to physical superiority, and the sixth is probably both economic and social in nature. So, though there are some definite differences in the attitudes of the two races on these matters, it would seem that there is a fuller understanding, or less significant divergence of opinion between the races with respect to the legal, educational, physical, and possibly economic status of the Negro as compared with the white than there is with respect to the social relationship between the two races. These facts are clearly evident in Table 3-II.*

Sex differences in opinion are of no major significance. Among the data which involve boys only, we note 67 differences, exclusive of "Don't Know" differences, which are as much as 3.83 times their

*The basic assumptions behind this table need to be understood. If on a given item 100 percent of the whites had said "True" or "Probably True," and 100 percent of the Negroes had said "False" or "Probably False," it is obvious that we have a situation which could be described as "100 percent disagreement." This would be arrived at by taking the percent by which the whites in the "True" and "Probably True" extreme exceeded the Negroes in that extreme, adding it to the percent by which the Negroes exceeded the white in the "False" and "Probably False" extreme, and dividing the total by two. In this same manner the percentages in this table are computed. Take the first item as an example. When the data of Table 3-I are studied it will be seen that 42 percent more Negroes than whites answered "True" or "Probably True." In turn, 36 percent more whites than Negroes answered "False" or "Probably False." When 42 percent and 36 percent are added, and the sum divided by two, the result is 39, which, in Table 3-II, is presented as the percent of difference in opinion on this item.

TABLE 3-II

PERCENT OF DIFFERENCE IN OPINION, WITH RESPECT TO
DESIGNATED ITEMS, BY SPECIFIED RACIAL GROUPS

Item	All Whites vs. All Negroes	White Boys vs. Negro Boys	White Girls vs. Negro Girls	Young Whites vs. Young Negroes	Older Whites vs. Older Negroes
1	39	39	40	37	39
2	12	4	2	2	4
3	34	31	33	27	43
4	51	57	46	47	52
5	38	42	43	32	40
6	33	38	28	29	36
7	40	40	40	34	54
8	69	70	69	62	80
9	23	22	23	19	31
10	24	21	17	14	21
11	35	29	35	32	35
12	21	23	21	19	20
13	13	25	13	20	31
14	15	17	15	15	15
15	46	45	46	39	53
16	46	41	46	47	41
17	46	43	46	39	53
18	21	25	21	21	19
19	12	11	12	7	4
20	76	75	76	72	80
21	41	50	41	44	49
22	63	71	63	66	71
23	44	44	44	35	41
24	40	40	40	34	43

probable error. This is to be compared with 71 such differences involving only girls. Naturally, this difference in the number of significant differences is too small to be significant. The fact that the girls show four more significant disagreements than the boys is offset by the fact that the mean percent of difference in Table 3-II is 35.8 for girls and 37.6 for boys. The fundamental comparability between the results for each sex separately is seen in a still further way when the percentages of disagreement of girls are correlated with those of boys. This results in a coefficient of 0.94, which when judged against the almost inconsequential difference in the means of the two groups, undoubtedly indicates that sex affiliation is not a matter of major importance in the determinaton of the racial attitudes of these students.

An analysis of the possible effect or influence of age on obtained differences was made by dividing both racial groups into those who were under 17 years of age, and those who were 17 years of age and older. This resulted in 313 young whites, and 147 older whites; 218 young Negroes, and 259 older Negroes. Probably the most apparent effect of the division is to show that there is, on the average, more difference in opinion between the older whites and older Negroes, than between the younger whites and younger Negroes. This is found in Table 3-II. The average percent of difference between the opinions of the younger groups is 33.88, and that between the older group is 39.80. On three of the items, number 16, 18, and 19, the younger groups show slightly, though very slightly, more disagreement. On one item, 16, the percent of difference was the same for both the younger and older groups. On 20 of the 24 items the older groups show more divergence of opinion than the younger groups. On six of the items, 7, 8, 9, 13, 15, and 17, the older groups showed more than 10 percent more disagreement than did the younger groups, the greatest increase with age, 20 percent, being on item 7. Strikingly, this pertains to the segregation of Negroes into separate schools, and is due almost entirely to a shift in opinion of the Negroes. The whites are almost alike in both age groups.

Item 8, a white man shaking hands with a Negro, shows a diverging opinion on the part of both whites and Negroes, but about 4 percent more shift on the part of Negroes than whites, Item 9, that of the two races working together on P.W.A and farm projects, results from a change in white opinion rather than from a shift among the Negroes. In fact, the latter group shows only a 1 percent change whereas the white group became about 15 percent more likely to oppose these interracial work projects.

On item 13, which pertains to the inability of Negroes to develop outstanding leaders, we have the interesting phenomenon of the whites becoming rather definitely more certain of the truth of the statement, and the Negroes becoming both more certain that it is true, and more certain that it is false. It would almost appear that whereas there is a growing trend on the part of Negroes, as they become older, to deny this, there also may be a kind of fatalistic acceptance of the idea on the part of others as they grow older.

Item 15 suggests that there should be no segregation of Negroes in picture shows. White opinion almost unanimously favors this in both age groups. It does shift from 93 to 97 percent in unqualified certainty, however. At the same time, Negro opinion shows a 12 percent shift in favor of the "open" show, with no segregation, as the groups become older.

Item 17, the using by Negroes of "Yes, sir" as opposed to "Yes" when addressing white men, shows about a 3 percent shift in white opinion, with the older whites accepting this somewhat more often than the younger. Among the Negroes, though, the older students were 13 percent more likely to reject this idea than were the younger ones. Among the remaining 14 items which show more difference of opinion among older students of the two races than the younger students, 12 reveal the fact that as the Negroes become older they changed their opinions more than did the whites.

The implications of a study such as this are almost as varied as the interests of different readers. Accordingly, the authors do not believe it to be incumbent upon them to impose their interests on those of the reader by drawing implications. In review, though, we would remind the reader that the study apparently indicates that attitudinal differences between the two racial groups, as here measured, are definitely more pronounced with respect to the social relations of the two groups than with respect to other factors measured. Second, it makes little difference whether it is a male or a female group which is being studied, each sex of each race holding to approximately the same attitudinal positions as the other sex of the same race. Lastly, instead of there being a "growing understanding" between the races, there is considerable evidence of a growing difference between them. Furthermore, this would appear to be due more toward a shift in Negro opinion than to a shift in white opinion, though shifts of this type are in evidence with both racial groups.

REFERENCES

1. BRYANT, G. E.: Recent trends in racial attitudes of Negro college students. *Journal of Negro Education, 10*:43-50, 1941.

2. DAVIS, T. E.: Some racial attitudes of Negro college and grade
   school students. *Journal of Negro Education, 6*:157-65, 1937.
3. BOLTON, E. R.: Measuring specific attitudes toward the social
   rights of the Negro. *J. Abnorm. Soc. Psychol., 37*:384-97, 1937.
4. BRALY, K., and KATZ, D.: Racial stereotypes of one hundred college students. *J. Abnorm. Soc. Psychol., 28*:280-90, 1933.
5. SMITH, M.: A comparison of white and Indian attitudes toward
   the Negro. *Journal of Negro Education, 6*:592-95, 1937.

Chapter 4

THE LEVELS OF ASPIRATION OF WHITE AND NEGRO CHILDREN IN A NONSEGREGATED ELEMENTARY SCHOOL

GEORGE FELIX BOYD

University of Oregon

During the past fifty years there has been a large number of studies which have dealt with differences between the Negro and the white man. However, few of these studies have been in areas not related to intelligence. It seems that few people are concerned with possible differences in attitudes which may be present in the two groups. The present project is meant to be one which will deal with this problem. It is assumed, however, that any differences found are the results of environmental factors and not innate "racial traits."

PROBLEM

The question which this study attempts to answer is whether or not there is a measurable difference in level of aspiration between white and Negro children of the same intelligence level in a nonsegregated elementary school.

Level of Aspiration

"The level of aspiration may be defined as an individual's goal or expectation in regard to the goodness of his own future performance in a given task"[2] (p 159). In other words, the level of aspiration is an individual's ambition in a dynamic situation.

Note. Reprinted by permission from *The Journal of Social Psychology*, *36*:191-196, 1952. The author wishes to thank his adviser, Dr. Leona Tyler, and Dr. Richard A. Littman for their aid and suggestions in this study. He would also like to express his sincere appreciation to Mr. and Mrs. L. A. Johnson and their son, Ben, for making his stay in Portland possible while the data for this study were being gathered.

Test situations involving the measurement of levels of aspiration are recent. Studies conducted by Hoppe and Dembo during the 1930's are among the first using test situations to measure levels of aspiration. Sears,[8,9] Gould,[4] Eysenck,[1] and Frank[2,3] are among the people who have since used test situations to measure level of aspiration.

Tests to measure levels of aspiration have varied considerably in their construction. They range from simple, timed, arthmetic and reading problems to problems involving various forms of muscular coordination. However, in spite of their dissimilarity in construction, all level-of-aspiration test situations must follow the same basic procedure: "A subject is confronted with some task and either before or after practice is asked to make a statement of how well he will do in the task. After failure or success in reaching this explicitly stated goal he is asked to make another estimate. This may be repeated several times"[6] (p 464).

Experimenters who have used level-of-aspiration test situations have not always agreed in their assumptions as to the meaning of this type of research. However, Rotter[6] (p 464) has "grouped these research studies into three divisions on the basis of their purposes. The first group is interested in determining principles applicable to the theory of personality. The second is interested mainly in the technique itself, its reliability, the generality of the response from one task to another, and the validity of the assumptions usually made in interpreting the results. The third group accepts the technique as a valid measuring device of some kind and uses it to study other variables." Thus, this present study is operating under the third assumption. In it the level-of-aspiration test situation is accepted "as a valid measuring device" to be used in the study of other variables.

PROCEDURES

The children for this study were selected from an elementary school in Portland, Oregon. A total of 50 were used; 25 were from each of the two racial groups. Each white child was paired with a Negro child of comparable economic status and *IQ* as measured by the Otis Quick-Scoring test. This was done to equate the groups rather than to compare the performance of each child with that of his paired partner.

The *IQ* of the white group ranged from 83 to 123, with a mean of 104.4. The Negro *IQ* ranged from 85 to 122, with a mean of 101.4. The mean ages for the Negro and white groups were 13 years, zero months, and 12 years, ten months, respectively. Thus, the groups were not only comparable in *IQ* and economic status but also in age.

Two tests and a questionnaire were used in this level-of-aspiration study. One of the tests was a target test and the other was an arithmetic test. The questionnaire consisted of 12 questions which were designed to get the child to verbalize his future hopes and plans.

In both the target and arithmetic tests the discrepancy score was used as the criterion since it seems to be the most adequate measure of level of aspiration. The discrepancy score is the difference between the actual preceding score and the stated expected score for the new trial. It is positive when the stated expected score is superior to the actual preceding performance score and negative when it is inferior. The data obtained from both tests received identical treatment. Means, standard deviations, and critical ratios were computed.

The questionnaire was administered in the form of an interview. This interview was "centered" around the child's opinion of the tests that he had taken, while the questions were apparently asked "in passing." The questionnaire data were treated quantitatively.

In no case were the children informed that the tests were to compare the two racial groups. Instead, the examiner told them that they were taking the tests in order to compare the abilities of boys with those of girls. This seemed to have stimulated a great deal of friendly rivalry between the boys and girls without regard to race.

RESULTS

The results obtained from this study seem to indicate that the Negro group has the higher level of aspiration. The critical ratio of the difference between the two groups on the target test is 2.46,

TABLE 4-I

THE TOTAL DISCREPANCY SCORES, MEAN DISCREPANCY SCORES,
AND STANDARD DEVIATIONS OF THE GROUPS ON THE
TARGET AND ARITHMETIC TESTS

	Total Discrepancy Score	Mean Discrepancy Score	Standard Deviation
(A) Target Test			
Negro	131.0	5.24	8.55
White	—12.0	—0.48	7.87
CR = 2.46			
(B) Arithmetic Test			
Negro	—5.0	—0.20	2.75
White	—56.0	—2.24	6.28
CR = 1.49			

which is significant at the 2 percent level. The difference between
the groups on the arithmetic test is not statistically significant,
but it is important since it points in the same direction as the
target test results. The critical ratio of the difference between the
groups on this test is 1.49, which is significant at the 14 percent
level (Table 4-I).

The data obtained from the questionnaire seem to indicate
that the Negro children are also higher than the white children
in their stated hopes and ambitions (see Table 4-II). They have
higher occupational ambitions, desire more foreign trips and larger
automobiles, and more Negro than white children stated that they
expect to be above-average students in high school. The mean
income desired by the white group is the higher, but the modes
of the two groups are the same and the Negro median is slightly
higher than the white. Six of the questions were of no discriminatory value.

DISCUSSION

The results of this study are probably contrary to the expectations of many people. However, if we look at a study by Gould,[4]
an adequate explanation may be found. In this study, which compares the levels of aspiration of students from a higher socioeconomic level with those of students from a relatively lower socioeconomic level, it was found that the lower socioeconomic group
had the higher level of aspiration. Gould suggests that these findings may be the results of feelings of insecurity which possibly

TABLE 4-II

A LISTING OF THE DISCRIMINATING DATA OBTAINED FROM THE
QUESTIONNARIES FOR BOTH GROUPS

	Negro	White
Occupational desires		
Doctors	1	
Dentists	1	
Nurses	4	1
Veterinarians		1
Geologists		1
Pilots		2
Clerical workers	4	1
Musicians	5	
Dramatists		1
Athletes	2	2
Movie actors	1	
Teachers	1	
Mechanics	2	1
Beauticians	1	
Waiters	1	1
Electricians	1	
Florists		1
Housewives		2
No idea	1	11
Educational ambitions		
Graduate and professional school	3	2
College graduates	18	16
Three years' college	2	
Two years' college	2	
Special school		1
High school only		6
Type of student expected to be in high school		
Average	18	21
Above average	7	3
Automobile choices		
Cadillacs	8	
Buicks	9	5
Lincolns	1	
Packards		1
Chryslers		2
Oldsmobiles	1	2
Mercurys	1	1
Hudsons	1	
Fords	1	5
Chevrolets	1	2
Studebakers		2
Plymouths		1
Trips desired		
Within U.S.A.	5	5
To U.S. territories	2	3
Foreign	13	10
Income desired		
Mean	$2,830	$3,075
Mode	$2,000	$2,000
Median	$2,025	$2,000

accompany a low socioeconomic status. A strong desire to improve one's conditions may be the result of insecure feelings. As a group, Negroes have a lower socioeconomic status than white Americans. It is therefore not strange that the Negro child possibly has similar feelings and needs to Gould's lower socioeconomic level group.

Another possible explanation of the higher Negro level of aspiration may be made in terms of adjustment to defeats and disappointment. The Negro child on the elementary school level may of necessity have better defense mechanisms against defeats and disappointment than his white schoolmate. As a result, the former may be more prone to set his goals very high because he realizes that he is prepared to adjust should he fail.

Some of the nondiscriminatory data obtained from the questionnaire seem to indicate that there is a large amount of "race pride" in the young Negro. Twenty-four of the 28 people selected by this group as the "greatest person in the world" and the "person to be like" are Negroes. This is very important when one realizes that these children have been reared in a society which has been dominated in almost every area by people who are not members of their race.

SUMMARY

The tests and questionnaire results in this study seem to indicate that the Negro group has a higher level of aspiration than the white group.

1. The critical ratio of the difference between the groups on the target test is 2.46 in favor of the Negro group. This is significant at the 2 percent level.

2. The difference between the groups on the arithmetic test is not significant but it points in the same direction as the target test results. The critical ratio of the difference on this test is 1.49. This is significant at the 14 percent level.

3. The Negro group has higher verbalized ambitions than the white group according to the questionnaire data.

REFERENCES

1. EYSENCK, H. J.: *Dimensions of Personality*. London, Routledge & Kegan Paul, 1947.

2. FRANK, J. D.: The influence of the level of performance in one task on the level of aspiration in another. *J. Exp. Psychol., 18*:159-171, 1935.
3. FRANK, J. D.: Recent studies of level of aspiration. *Psychol. Bull., 38*:218-226, 1941.
4. GOULD, R.: Some sociological determinants of goal strivings. *J. Soc. Psychol., 13*:461-473, 1941.
5. KLINEBERG, O.: *Negro Intelligence and Selective Migration.* New York, Columbia U. Pr., 1947.
6. ROTTER, J. B.: Level of aspiration as a method of studying personality: I. A critical review of methodology. *Psychol. Rev., 49*: 463-473, 1942.
7. ROTTER, J. B.: Level of aspiration as a method of studying personality: IV. The analysis of patterns of response. *J. Soc. Psychol., 21*:159-177, 1945.
8. SEARS, P. S.: Levels of aspiration in academically successful and unsuccessful children. *J. Abnorm. Soc. Psychol., 35*:498-536, 1940.
9. SEARS, P.S.: The level of aspiration in relation to some variables of personality: Clinical studies. *J. Soc. Psychol., 14*:311-336, 1941.
10. TYLER, L. E.: *The Psychology of Human Differences.* New York, D. Appleton Century, 1947.
11. VAN DEUSEN, J. G.: *The Black Man in White America.* Washington, D.C., Associated Publishers, 1944.

Chapter 5

CHILDREN'S PERCEPTIONS OF THE SOCIAL ROLES OF NEGROES AND WHITES

Marian J. Radke and Helen G. Trager

Bureau for Intercultural Education, New York City

PURPOSE

The purpose of this research was to study the extent to which young children are aware of social differences and to determine the part which social differences play in the development of children's attitudes toward race.

The racial attitudes expressed by children* which hold a race in contempt ("I hate colored," "Nigger men are dirty") or which regard a race with fear ("Whites kill colored," "Colored carry knives") or which boast of a superiority of one over the other

Note. Reprinted by permission from *The Journal of Psychology, 29*:3-33, 1950. Also published as a separate. Copyright by The Journal Press.

The formulation of this research was begun with the collaboration of the late Dr. Kurt Lewin. The authors wish to express their indebtedness to his help and inspiration. Grateful acknowledgment is made to Professors Louis Raths and Avrum Ben-Avi, both of the School of Education, New York University, for detailed criticism of the manuscript, and staff members Hadassah Davis, Eleanor Kelly, Elizabeth Purnell, Alice Togo, and Benjamin Goldenberg for their invaluable assistance.

The Philadelphia Early Childhood Project was made possible through the co-operation of the Philadelphia public schools; the Bureau for Intercultural Education, New York; the Research Center for Group Dynamics, Massachusetts Institute of Technology, and the Philadelphia Fellowship Commission. Helen Trager of the Bureau for Intercultural Education is project director; C. Leslie Cushman of the Philadelphia public schools is responsible for administrative arrangements within the schools; Marian Radke of the Research Center is responsible for scientific supervision; and Mary V. Thompson, a collaborating teacher of the Philadelphia public schools, is supervisor of classroom activities.

*Quotations are from a study reported in *Genetic Psychology Monographs,* November, 1949, "Social Perceptions and Attitudes of Children," by Marian J. Radke, Helen G. Trager, and Hadassah Davis.[1]

("Whites is better than colored") are products of a culture which gives many evidences of interracial antagonisms linked with social and economic factors. Do these social factors (such as housing, employment, education, and segregation in social life) play an important role in the development of the child's image of and attitude toward each race?

This study of young children is concerned with their comprehension of and interpretation of social roles of Negroes and whites: (a) Are Negroes and whites perceived in terms of social, economic, and occupational roles? (b) What inferences are made from the perceived roles? As one of the factors in a child's reactions toward a race, role distinctions may become the supporting reasons or rationalizations for hostility or friendliness, or may actually give rise to the feelings of acceptance or rejection, or inferiority or superiority. The quick generalization about a group from a specific experience, the interpretation of all events in terms of a single false stereotype about a group is familiar in adult life. Is it the same for a child? Does the white child who has seen Negro women doing menial work or has seen Negroes living in a poor neighborhood generalize that all Negro women necessarily do menial work, and that all Negroes necessarily live in poor neighborhoods? Are valuations of the Negro race made on the basis of these stereotypes: they don't do better work because they don't care or don't know any better; they don't live in better homes because they are dirty or don't appreciate nicer things? Thus, it is not only a question of whether or not social differences are recognized by children but also of how these differences enter into the origins and maintenance of prejudice.

SAMPLE

Two hundred and forty-two children* from kindergarten, first, and second grades in six Philadelphia public schools were tested. There were 90 Negro children and 152 white children. The children are from middle and lower socioeconomic levels, the greatest proportion from the lower-middle and upper-lower groups. The racial composition of the six neighborhoods varies: one school

---

*The children in this report are the same subjects whose attitudes toward Negro and white races were studied through the use of picture materials and interviews.[1]

and neighborhood has an all white population; three neighborhoods are predominantly white with from 5 percent to 10 percent Negro population; and the fifth and sixth neighborhoods have 90 percent to 95 percent Negro population (one of these schools has 100 percent Negro population).

The sample was selected by taking every third child on the class lists. Each child was interviewed alone, the white children by a white examiner, the Negro children by a Negro examiner.

METHOD

The child's perceptions of the social roles of Negro and white adults and his valuations of members of each race were investigated through the use of doll materials and an interview. The testing procedure creates choice situations involving Negro and white dolls and story-telling about the dolls—the stories structured by the examiner to involve social roles or circumstances of the persons represented by the dolls.

Instrument

The materials consist of plywood formboards with the cut-out figure of a man or a woman, plywood clothes to fit the figures, and plywood forms of houses.* Each formboard has an eight-inch figure of a man or woman. The head, hands, and feet for the man figure and the head, arms, and legs for the woman figure are painted on the board and the outline of the suit or dress is cut out. In the test situation a pair of formboards (two men dolls for boy subjects, two women dolls for girl subjects) are presented to the subject. The figures on the boards are identical except that one is given "brown" skin color and the other "white" skin color. Costume insets representing "dress-up," "work," and "shabby" clothes which fit into the cut-out areas are presented with the formboard figures. The three variations of costumes are in duplicate so that the same kind of costume can be given to both dolls. Each costume was intended to suggest variations in role (social, economic, and occupational). Objectively, the costumes appear

---

*Test materials were constructed by William Vitarelli of Teachers College, Columbia University, pursuant to the plans of the authors.

thus: The man's "dress-up" clothes are a neat, dark blue suit, white shirt, and red tie; his "work" clothes are a blue "denim"-color shirt, no jacket, no tie, and blue-grey trousers; and his "shabby" clothes are a faded, wrinkled, grey-blue suit, soiled white shirt not tucked in, and a faded, twisted, and loose tie. The woman's "dress-up" clothes are a blue dress trimmed with a narrow edging of yellow with red and white dots; her "work" clothes are a blue-green house dress with white collar and a neat white apron tied around the waist; and her "shabby" clothes are faded grey-green, ill-fitting blouse and skirt, skirt buttoned carelessly, blouse buttoned and pinned, and both blouse and skirt wrinkled.

Pretesting, as well as the responses of the children in the study, establish the meaning of the costumes to the children to be as follows. Activities associated with dress-up clothes are sharply distinguished from those associated with work or shabby clothes. For a majority of both boys and girls, dress-up clothes suggest "going out," visiting, shopping, dancing, or going to church. Both work and shabby clothes are generally seen as appropriate for working. The woman's work clothes are almost always associated with doing housework (cooking, cleaning, and such), and her shabby clothes with doing housework or staying around the house; similarly, the man's work and shabby clothes are most frequently associated with working or "staying around home." To a small number of the children, shabby clothes suggest disreputable status or activities—"drunk," "hanging around" (see Table 5-I).

The houses in the test are painted on plywood boards (about $12'' \times 18''$). On one board are two identical one-family houses of red brick with white trim (fairly typical of middle-class and lower-class houses in the community of the children tested). Each house has a small front lawn and trees in the background. On the other board are two multiple dwellings of red-brown color, separated by an alley, and having a run-down appearance of a city slum—a clothes line, overflowing ash cans.

Administration of the Test

The child is brought to this test after an interview in which he was required to respond to pictures of groups of children of different races and religions. He has been asked to interpret the

ACTIVITIES DESCRIBED FOR EACH COSTUME BY NEGRO AND WHITE CHILDREN

TABLE 5-I

ACTIVITIES DESCRIBED FOR EACH COSTUME BY NEGRO AND WHITE CHILDREN
(Percentage of Children)

	"Dress-up"				"Work"				"Shabby"			
	Negro Girls	White Girls	Negro Boys	White Boys	Negro Girls	White Girls	Negro Boys	White Boys	Negro Girls	White Girls	Negro Boys	White Boys
Going out	63	67	66	52	6	5	26	17	9	22	7	9
Going to party, movies, church	21	5	16	19	—	—	7	2	—	—	0	1
Dressing up, good clothes	16	2	0	7	—	—	—	—	3	0	—	—
A uniform	—	—	5	6	—	—	—	7	—	—	—	2
Playing, having fun	—	6	2	8	—	14	2	7	4	5	0	—
Working, going to work	0	13	—	—	3	71	52	43	9	8	64	51
Housework	0	—	—	—	91	3	—	—	34	50	—	—
Maid dress	—	—	—	—	0	—	—	—	—	—	—	—
Staying home	—	—	—	—	—	1	9	10	38	6	11	10
Old, wrinkled, dirty, ragged	—	—	—	—	0	—	1	7	3	0	7	8
Drunk, jail, fighting	—	—	—	—	—	—	—	—	0	1	4	6
Miscellaneous, don't know	0	7	11	8	0	6	3	14	0	8	7	13

situations portrayed in the pictures and to describe the meanings of religious and racial differences observed.

The test reported here was separated from the preceding interview by an intermission during which the child was free to do as he liked. This test was introduced as "a game we are going to play," and the materials were presented as follows. The three pairs of costumes are placed in a row in front of the child with identical costumes placed one on the other. Left to right order to the child are "dress-up," "work," and "shabby" costumes. The male doll is used for the boys, and the female doll for the girls. The examiner asks "Do you know what these toys are?" and then, to reaffirm the child's response or to establish the fact, says:

> Yes, they're different kinds of clothes. What would a man (woman) be doing if he were wearing these clothes? (pointing one at a time in the left to right order).

After the child has said what each costume means to him, he is asked which he likes best, and why.

The dolls (formboards) are then presented. The questioning proceeds as follows:

> Now let's look at these dolls. We have two men. What do you think—are they just alike or are they different?

If the child answers "different" he is asked how they are different. These questions are frankly intended to have the child acknowledge the racial (color) difference. The examiner says:

> This is a colored man and this is a white man. Now let's dress these men. You put on their clothes. Any one will fit; they are all the same size.

After the child has put clothes on both dolls, he is asked:

> What would this man be doing wearing these clothes? Can you tell me a story about the man? (Tester points first to the Negro doll and then to the white doll.)

The clothes are then taken off the dolls and the examiner suggests "Let's dress them again." The same questions are asked as in the first choice, and also "Which man do you like best? Why?"

The dolls are left as last dressed, the extra costumes are removed, and the examiner presents the houses, with the following questions:

> Here are some houses. Which do you like best?
> In which house does the colored man live? Why do you think so?
> In which house does the white man live? Why do you think so?
> Do you think these two men are friends?
> Which house is like your house?

The child can assign both dolls to the same kind of houses (there are two houses of each kind) or one doll to a "good" house and one doll to a "poor" house. That the two houses of a given kind are next to one another may affect the choices of children who are aware of racial segregation in housing.

The data were analyzed with reference to the following research questions: (a) Is an awareness of social class distinction between Negroes and whites revealed in responses to the play materials and the questions? (b) What kinds of affective reactions and stereotyping are apparent in the responses? (c) How do the children's responses on this test compare with their responses to the earlier picture test of attitudes? (d) How do the responses vary with the race and age of the children?

Retest Reliability of the Responses

Forty-two children were retested three weeks later. Reactions on the two occasions of testing are discussed in the analysis in relation to specific test questions.

ANALYSIS OF THE DATA

In a restricted choice situation such as that imposed by this test, many variations in attitude and understanding concerning Negro and white races have no chance for expression. Their loss of data is justified only if, by a highly structured and directed situation, it is possible to study in greater detail some special aspects of the problem. In this study, the special aspects in focus are the children's understanding of social evidences of race prejudice: the favored and less favored social, economic, and occupational circumstances of the white and Negro populations. The role which these social factors play in children's images of and attitudes toward race may be revealed in their choices of clothes and houses for the dolls of each race and in their explanations or stories about their choices.

Reaction to Dolls

To establish the fact of difference between the dolls, the children were asked "Are they the same or different?" "Tell me how they are different." Virtually all the children say that the dolls are different (99 percent of the Negro children, 92 percent of the white children), and most children make the difference explicitly that of color (79 percent and 77 percent of Negro and white children respectively). The white children tend to be more explicit in stating color as meaning racial distinctions. This response increases with age in both groups (Table 5-II). The children retested give almost identical responses on both tests (90 percent responded in the same way on both tests).

After the child's response to the question on difference, the examiner reiterated the color distinction between the dolls before going on with the test.

Clothes Chosen for Negro and White Dolls and Activities Ascribed to Each Doll

The converse of the theory that "clothes make the man" might lead one to expect that the choice of costumes for Negro and white dolls would reflect the child's conception of what clothes are appropriate to each race. The explanations accompanying such assignments should reveal partly the extent to which the child's perceptions of race have differentiations in terms of social roles.

TABLE 5-II

	Percentage of					
	Negro Children			*White Children*		
	Kgn.	*1st Grade*	*2nd Grade*	*Kgn.*	*1st Grade*	*2nd Grade*
One's a white man, one's a colored man	33	34	58	33	44	70
One's a "nigger" (and similar distinctions)	0	0	0	5	8	0

Since the costumes in the test do not represent any one role or activity (for example, the dress with apron could represent "mother" as well as "maid"), the child must bring to the test his own associations.

Since the children tested are from the middle, lower-middle, and lower economic classes, they are not likely to experience first-hand in their neighborhoods such gross inequities between Negroes and whites in income, occupations, and housing as exist in some parts of society. However, even without a sharp contrast existing in reality for many of the subjects, these children show an awareness that derives from adult attitudes in their immediate environment, reinforced by stereotypes in comics, movies, radio, and tabloids.

The choices of costumes for each doll are given in Table 5-III. These data show the influence of the "race" of the doll and the race of the child responding. At each age level, white and Negro

TABLE 5-III

COSTUMES ASSIGNED TO NEGRO AND WHITE DOLLS
(Percentage of Children)
A. *Assignments to Each Doll*

Doll	Costume	Negro Children				White Children			
		Kgn.	1st Grade	2nd Grade	Total	Kgn.	1st Grade	2nd Grade	Total
Negro	Dress-up	68	78	88	78	38	32	20	30
	Work	18	13	6	12	22	23	31	25
	Shabby	14	9	6	10	40	45	49	45
White	Dress-up	28	31	31	30	42	52	68	54
	Work	43	47	52	47	34	37	20	30
	Shabby	29	22	17	23	24	11	12	16

B. *Pairs of Assignments*

Costume Assigned		Negro Children				White Children			
To Negro Doll	To White Doll	Kgn.	1st Grade	2nd Grade	Total	Kgn.	1st Grade	2nd Grade	Total
Dress-up	Dress-up	13	16	23	17	12	6	0	6
Dress-up	Work	26	47	48	41	7	20	10	12
Dress-up	Shabby	26	16	17	20	20	6	10	12
Work	Dress-up	9	6	3	6	12	16	29	19
Work	Work	13	0	3	5	10	5	0	5
Work	Shabby	0	6	0	2	0	2	2	2
Shabby	Dress-up	13	9	6	9	17	29	39	28
Shabby	Work	0	0	0	0	17	13	10	13
Shabby	Shabby	0	0	0	0	5	3	0	3

TABLE 5-IV

Preferred Costume	By Negro Children	By White Children
Dress-up	96%	85%
Work	2%	10%
Shabby	2%	5%

children dress the dolls differently; both favor the doll of their own race. When asked "Which do you like best?" the choices of costumes are as indicated in Table 5-IV. In the assignment of these preferred costumes, favoritism to own race is as indicated in Table 5-V. The bias increases with age among both Negro and white children.

Negro children are much more emphatic about dressing-up the doll representing their own race (78 percent in dress-up compared to 22 percent in work and shabby clothes) than are the white children (54 percent in dress-up and 46 percent in work and shabby clothes). Both races tend to avoid giving the same kind of clothes to both dolls (Part B, Table 5-III). This combination appears most often when Negro children give dress-up clothes to both dolls (17 percent). If the costumes are considered as having a rank order of preference with dress-up first, work second, and shabby third, both Negro and white children tend to choose pairs in which their own group has the higher rank order of preference (Table 5-VI).

The data in Table 5-III give little evidence of awareness by the children of differences in the social roles or status of Negroes and whites. It can be concluded either (a) that these aspects of society are not noticed by children, or (b) that the test materials are not appropriate stimuli to call forth role differences. These two possibilities are investigated in the analysis of activities ascribed to the dolls. But before examining these responses within Table 5-III, some exceptions may be taken to the generalization

TABLE 5-V

Preferred Costume	By Negro Children				By White Children			
Assigned to	Kgn.	1st	2nd	Total	Kgn.	1st	2nd	Total
Negro doll	61%	72%	89%	74%	32%	40%	18%	30%
White doll	26%	28%	31%	28%	47%	55%	63%	55%

TABLE 5-VI

White children choose combinations of:	
Dress-up for white doll and work or shabby for Negro doll	47 percent of the cases
Work for white doll and shabby for Negro doll	13 percent of the cases
Negro children do the same for their group, giving:	
Dress-up for Negro doll and work or shabby for white doll	61 per cent of the cases
Work for Negro doll and shabby for white doll	2 percent of the cases

above. That the Negro children (78 percent) consistently give greater emphasis than the white children (54 percent) to dressing-up the doll of their own race suggests their greater sensitivity to the social significance of clothes. It is possible, too, that the choices of work and shabby clothes for the white doll by the Negro children (70 percent) are partly retaliatory in nature. These reactions of the Negro children, if not expressing role differences directly, may well stem from an awareness of these differences. The differences in costumes seem of less importance to the white children,* although there is an increase with age in both groups.

The questions "What would this man be doing wearing these clothes?" or "Can you tell me a story about this man?" were designed to discover whether children associated particular occupations with either race. The phrasing of the questions, however, stimulated children to discuss specific activities instead of occupations. Nevertheless, the children's perceptions of Negroes' and whites' roles in society emerge clearly (Table 5-VII). Again, the responses of Negro and white children differ. Considering first the white children, about half describe similar activities or roles for both dolls, suggesting no preference or advantage for one over the other. Forty-two percent, however, create very unequal situations in which the activity of the white doll is distinctly more desirable than that of the Negro doll. These responses range from stereotyped social roles linked with race in which the Negro is given the lower status, to unequally pleasant activities or occupa-

*Retest of 38 children showed low agreement between the costumes chosen for either doll: 60 percent chose the same costumes for the Negro doll on both tests, 76 percent for the white doll.

TABLE 5-VII

DESCRIBED ACTIVITIES FOR NEGRO AND WHITE DOLLS
(Percentage of Children)

	Negro Children	White Children
A. Specific advantaged social or occupational role for white and low status role for Negro	0	14
B. Specific advantaged social or occupational role for Negro and low status role for white	1	1
C. Work role for Negro and leisure role for white	8	24
D. Work role for white and leisure role for Negro	37	6
E. More desirable of two occupations given to white	0	2
F. More desirable of two occupations given to Negro	0	1
G. More pleasant of two activities given to white	0	2
H. More pleasant of two activities given to Negro	5	1
I. Same or similar occupations given to both	10	22
J. Same or similar activities given to both	39	27

tions which do not specify a definite social role. About 10 percent of the responses of the white children describe the more pleasant activity or occupation for the Negro doll. The content of each of these categories of response in Table 5-VIII is described below.

Social and occupational role stereotypes given by 14 percent of the white children correspond closely to the stereotypes in adult society. Illustrations which follow are the most frequently given types of distinctions in roles:

First grader: (Negro doll given shabby costume; white doll, dress-up) "She [Negro doll] could be cleaning; all ladies who are colored are maids." "She [white doll] had a child [for whom she went out] to buy shoes."

Second grader: (Negro doll given work costume; white doll, shabby) [Negro doll] "maid in house. Take care of child." [White doll] "going uptown to dance."

First grader: (Negro doll given shabby costume; white doll, dress-up) "She's [Negro doll] a nigger working in the house." "She's [White doll] out buying food, comes home and changes dress."

Second grader: (Negro doll given work costume; white doll,

TABLE 5-VIII

	First	Second
Both dolls in dress-up clothes	18%	3%
Negro doll in dress-up and white doll in work or shabby clothes	61%	3%
Both dolls in work or shabby clothes	6%	5%
Negro doll in work or shabby and white doll in dress-up clothes	15%	27%

dress-up) "She's [Negro doll] a maid and minds the children while she [white] is out." "She [white doll] goes out and has a good time."

First grader: (Negro doll given dress-up; white doll, work) "She's [Negro doll] going to Sunday School or to hospital to see her kids."

"The colored lady is cooking for her [white doll]."

In the last quotation, even though the clothes assigned make it more likely that the white woman would be working, the Negro woman is given the servant role. Thus, while social status factors did not appear in the choices of clothes by the white children, social status differences are verbalized in their description of activities for the persons represented by the dolls.

Racial distinctions made by the white boys do not involve a servant role, but more frequently, the boys who recognize status factors mention the limited work opportunities of the Negro man:

First grader: (Negro doll given work costume; white doll, dress-up) [Negro doll] "is hanging around. He doesn't have no work." [White doll] "going uptown shopping."

Or the likelihood of the Negro's doing more menial work than the white man:

Second grader: (Negro doll given shabby costume; white doll, dress-up) "He [Negro doll] would be digging dirt." "He [white doll] would be going on a vacation."

Four percent of the white children (included in category *A*, Table 5-VII) differentiate on the grounds of what might be called the moral status of Negroes and whites, indicating in each case less desirable behavior from the Negro, thus:

Second grader: "The colored [Negro doll] don't believe in God." "They [white doll] believes in God and goes to church."

First grader: "They [Negro doll] are gangsters; that's what they look like." "He's [white doll] going out to buy his mother some presents."

Second grader: (Negro doll given shabby costume; white doll, work) [Negro doll] "is coming out of a jail." [White doll] "is taking a walk." "He is a Negro and he is a white, but he doesn't like him. He is black and is Chinese, but this one [white] is an American."

Not unlike prejudiced adults, the child quoted above combines into one category all people or qualities which he discards—"Negro," "black," "Chinese"—and into another category all which he accepts—"white," "American."

Many more responses of white children involve a status difference in which racial factors are not verbalized. Thus, 24 percent of the white children ascribe work to the Negro man or woman and leisure activities to the white man or woman:

> *Second grader:* (Negro doll given shabby costume; white, dress-up) "I guess he'd [Negro doll] be going to work." "He'd [white doll] be going to the movies with his wife."
>
> *Kindergartener:* (Negro doll given work costume; white doll, dress-up) "She's [Negro doll] doing housework." "She's [white doll] going to the movies."

The cases (9 percent) in which the Negro man or woman is given the better of two activities or occupations (categories *B, D, F, H,* Table 5-VII) do not specify race in the responses. Thus, the Negro doll is described as "going out" or "walking along the street" or "going into a restaurant and thinking what he can buy for Christmas . . ." and, in contrast, the white doll is seen as "washing dishes," "coming home from work and his wife cooks for him," "working on a farm." Only one child describes a specific low-status role to the white woman, that of "maid," while the Negro woman is "going to a party."

While most of the activities classified as the same or similar for both dolls do not involve racial identifications of the dolls, a few (4 percent of the whtie boys) bring in themes of racial hostility. An example of this follows:

The two dolls are included in the same story thus:

> This was once a colored man. Both having fights. The white man beat the colored. . . . He [Negro] gave this guy a sore. He [white] beat up the other guy. See the blood, *see!*

Similar, though less vivid, descriptions of aggression appear in several of the responses of Negro children.

As in the case of the white children, Negro children's answers to "What would the man (woman) be doing?" do not conform to the impression given by their choices of costumes. While showing overwhelming favor for the Negro doll in choice of clothes, however, 49 percent of the Negro children assign similar activities to both dolls; only 43 percent give more desirable activities to the Negro doll; and 8 percent describe work for the Negro and leisure for the white doll.

To what extent these responses represent wish level or reality level may be gauged partly from a consideration of the following data. Few of the Negro children (19 percent—see categories *A, B, C, E, F, I,* Table 5-VII) describe work of any kind for the Negro doll. It is given, instead, activities such as going to church, to the movies, and down town, which do not involve a comparison of social status. The predominance of these responses may represent an avoidance of comparisons with the white doll which show Negroes at a disadvantage. If this interpretation is correct, then avoidance, rather than unawareness, may explain too the very small proportion of Negro children who ascribe the stereotyped "service" roles to the Negro man or woman.

Responses in category *D* of Table 5-VII, in which the white doll is made to work while the Negro is given leisure, are undoubtedly motivated at least for some of the children by wishful thinking and denial of hard reality in their own family situations. Such would seem to be the case of several Negro children whose mothers are in fact employed as domestics. These responses are illustrated by the following:

> *First grader:* (Negro doll given dress-up; white doll, shabby) [Negro doll] "goes out to store and friend's house." [White doll] "scrubs, washes, irons."

The children were asked to assign costumes and activities to the dolls a second time. The choice situation at the second request may appear somewhat different from the first. The directive "Dress the dolls again" does not necessarily invite the child to use exactly the same costumes that he has used earlier. He is likely to react to the need to use all the play materials provided or he may, also, interpret the second request as meaning that his first choices were "incorrect." Trends from first to second questioning suggest certain factors influencing the changes made. The responses of the Negro children on first and second questioning are given in Table 5-VIII (in percentages). The largest shift is in the direction of giving both dolls the work or shabby costumes, instead of giving them to the white doll and putting dress-up clothes on the Negro doll as in the first response. The motivations, however, on both occasions may be the same: in both cases the white doll is given the less desirable of the costumes available. Either the influence of social reality (apparent in responses on houses), which is the relatively poor economic circumstances of the Negro children studied, or a felt need to use the other play materials may account for the increased number of Negro dolls also given work or shabby clothes. However, neither kind of influence changes the Negro children's choices for the white doll.

The descriptions of activities follow the same pattern of change. Whereas 43 percent of the Negro children initially described a leisure or superior role for the Negro doll and a work role for the white doll, only 5 percent do so on second questioning. Most of the second descriptions are of equivalent activities for both dolls.

Responses of the white children on second questioning do not change as much, but show the same trend as in the responses of the Negro children toward a greater use of work or shabby clothes for both dolls (in percentages, Table 5-IX). However, the trend is nullified by the activities ascribed to the dolls. They are substantially the same as those reported in Table 5-VII in which the white doll continues to have the favored or superior role in about two fifths of the cases.

Thus, awareness of inequalities of social status is manifested in the children's responses to the test materials of clothing—manifested differently, however, by the Negro and white children. The white children tend to be more outspoken in creating specific advantaged and disadvantaged roles for the white and Negro dolls respectively. The Negro children give many indirect indications

TABLE 5-IX

	First	Second
Both dolls in dress-up clothes	6%	7%
Negro doll in dress-up, white doll in work or shabby clothes	24%	22%
Both dolls in work or shabby clothes	22%	48%
Negro doll in work or shabby, white doll in dress-up clothes	48%	23%

of sensitivity and awareness through denial, retaliation, and ambi-
valence.

Houses Chosen for Negro and White Dolls and Reasons Given for Choices

Another area in which there are obvious inequities in our
society between Negroes and whites is housing. Different kinds
of houses were presented and the subject was asked to assign each
doll to a house and to give his reasons for the assignments: "Here
are some houses. Which do you like best?" "In which house does
the colored man live? Why do you think so?" "In which house
does the white man live? Why do you think so?"

As in the case of the costumes, two "good" houses and two
"poor" houses were shown so that assignment of one doll did not
preclude assignment of the other doll to the same type of house.
On the other hand, the fact that the two "good" houses and the
two "poor" houses were contiguous may have encouraged the subjects to assign the dolls to different types of houses if they were
responding to a pattern of segregated housing. This was implied
occasionally in a child's reasons.

The data establish beyond all doubt that race differences play
a significant part in the reactions to the houses. Association of
white doll with good houses (the preferred houses by almost all
of the subjects) and Negro doll with poor houses is well established
among children of both races (Table 5-X). Eighty-two percent of
the white children assign the poor house to the Negro doll; only

TABLE 5-X

RESPONSES TO GOOD AND POOR HOUSES
(Percentage of Children)

	House Assigned to Negro Doll:		House Assigned to White Doll:		House Identified as Like Own:		
	Good	Poor	Good	Poor	Good	Poor	Neither
Negro children							
Kindergarten	35	65	48	52	17	61	22
1st grade	34	66	59	41	34	41	25
2nd grade	31	69	74	26	17	40	43
Total	33	67	60	40	23	47	30
White children							
Kindergarten	27	73	66	34	19	15	66
1st grade	14	86	81	19	24	32	44
2nd grade	12	88	85	15	18	47	35
Total	18	82	77	23	21	31	48

TABLE 5-XI

Same assignment of white doll by white children	65 percent of the cases
Same assignment of Negro doll by white children	73 percent of the cases
Same assignment of Negro doll by Negro children	53 percent of the cases
Same assignment of white doll by Negro children	65 percent of the cases

23 percent assign the poor house to the white doll ($x^2=80.84$, 1 percent level of significance). The Negro children respond by assigning the poor house to the Negro doll in 67 percent of the cases and to the white doll in 40 percent of the cases ($x^2=15.05$, 1 percent level of significance). The good house is given predominantly to the white doll (by 77 percent of the white children and 60 percent of the Negro children).

There is an increase with age in choice of the good house for the white doll by the white children, and similarly in choice of poor house for Negro doll. Neither trend is statistically significant. The Negro children show an increase with age only in the choice of the good house for the white doll, but this trend too is not statistically significant.

In the group of children retested after three weeks the results were as indicated in Table 5-XI. The lower agreement for the Negro children may indicate their greater conflict, their response depending on whether wishful thinking or the reality situations is most potent at the moment of choice.

The reasons for selecting houses for the dolls show how racial factors affect the reactions (Table 5-XII). The responses run the

TABLE 5-XII

REASONS FOR ASSIGNING DOLLS TO HOUSES
(Percentages of Children)

House Assigned	Reasons Given	Negro Doll		White Doll	
		Negro Children	White Children	Negro Children	White Children
Good house					
A.	Explicit stereotypes of racial status	0	2	4	11
B.	Implied stereotypes of racial status:				
	Because it is clean, nice, pretty, etc.	8	3	8	31
	Because he is white (Negro)	1	0	9	7
C.	Nondescript, miscellaneous	24	12	41	29
Poor house					
A.	Explicit stereotypes of racial status	5	17	1	2
B.	Implied stereotypes of racial status:				
	Because it is ugly, old, dirty, etc.	9	22	3	2
	Because he is white (Negro)	3	3	2	0
C.	Nondescript, miscellaneous	50	41	32	18

gamut from elaborate stereotypes and generalizations to comments
eloquent in the unstated implications. A fairly large proportion of
the children are inarticulate and vague (category *C*). White children most frequently rationalize putting the white doll in the good
house by such assertions as "White ladies has their houses cleaner,"
"'Cause white lady has more money and white fixes up her house
better than colored" (category *A*), or by statements which imply
these stereotypes (category *B*), as "Because it is more brighter and
the grass is nice and the man cuts it." Similiar responses are given
by 21 percent of the Negro children, though many more Negro
children give nondescript answers.

When white children put the Negro doll in the poor house they
support their choice with such reasons as:

> That's the way the colored man live; they live in sloppy
> houses.
> Because colored people don't keep their houses so neat.
> Because colored people don't take care of their houses.
> Because it is dirty and all colored live dirty.
> Colored man live in houses like this—a shabby thing.
> 'Cause they keep windows and doors open. Sometimes can't
> believe they're colored, they're so nice.
> All the colored live in beat up houses.
> Riding on trolley we see most colored people houses aren't
> painted right and pavements are sloppy.

The unstated assumptions so apparent in category *B*, in which 25
percent of the white children fall, are illustrated by:

> Because he lives in old houses.
> Because all broken down.
> Because it's ugly.

In assigning the Negro doll to the poor house, the Negro children are seldom articulate. The few (17 percent) whose reasons
are not "out of the field" ("He goes to the movies" or "The house
is green") or avoidant ("Because") give generalizations about Negroes' social status, illustrated by the following examples:

> Colored men are poorer than white.
> 'Cause his house ain't good as the white man house.
> He may not have much money.

When the Negro doll is given the good house by either white

or Negro children, the reason is usually nondescript: "Because he likes to" (white child).

A very few are definite and suggest an ideology about race, stating that because it is the nicer house they want it for the colored doll, thus: "Because I like pretty houses for colored" (white child), "It's nice and he's colored" (Negro child).

One white kindergarten child assigns the Negro doll to the good house because "She is the maid there."

Reasons for assigning the white doll to the poor house are usually irrelevancies ("Because it is red"). Two percent of the white children and 3 percent of the Negro children say that its being "old," "ugly," and so on is the reason it belongs to the white doll.

Interpretation of responses to the houses depends somewhat upon knowing the kinds of housing which Negroes and whites have in the environments of these children. Three sets of data have been compared: (a) the child's identification of his own house as like or different from the houses in the test (Table 5-X), (b) the actual housing in the neighborhoods, and (c) the houses selected for the dolls.

The white children describe their own housing as follows: about one fifth select the good house as like their own, one third select the poor house, and one half say neither is like their own. For the white children as a whole, these proportions are not grossly in error when compared with their neighborhoods.

Negro children identify their own house with the good house in 23 percent of the cases and with the poor house in 47 percent. Compared with housing in their neighborhoods this is an under selection of the poor house and over selection of the good house. It is likely that there is considerable ego involvement by the Negro children in identifying their own house after many of them have put the white doll in the good house and the Negro doll in the poor house and have given reasons (about 25 percent of the Negro children) which state or imply uncomplimentary stereotypes about Negroes. Is it then a combination of reality and cultural stereotypes which accounts for the reactions of the 47 percent of Negro children who identify the poor house as like their own, and who also put the Negro doll in the poor house? These responses contrast with their tendency to dress-up the Negro doll. It may be that housing constitutes a more permanent and unhappy aspect of their living than clothes, and so housing acquires early a "racial" significance and finality which does not exist in matters of clothes. Cultural stereotypes or experience with housing beyond their immediate neighborhoods most probably account for the responses of many of the Negro children who put the white doll in the good house in contrast to the Negro doll in the poor house. Housing of white families in the neighborhoods of these Negro children does not always contrast with the housing of Negro families.

Thirty percent of the Negro children do not compare their own house with the test houses. For at least a portion of these children, this response represents an avoidance of the situation. For others, it is in line with reality in that they live in houses which are better than those pictured, but unlike the kind of good house in the test.

The choice of the good house by 23 percent includes two types of response: the same reaction indicated above as well as a wishful response, a desire to have a good house.

While having shown more reality than the Negro children in answering which house is like the one in which they live, the white children in their placement of Negro and white dolls are not so much influenced by the nature of their own houses or neighborhoods. The stereotype or feeling of contrast in the circumstances of whites and Negroes appear to determine their response. Thus, 77 percent of the white children put the white doll in the good house, whereas only 21 percent say the good house is like their own. Among the 31 percent of white children who say that the poor house is like their own, 77 percent of them, nevertheless, give the Negro doll the poor and the white doll the good house in the test.

Feelings Expressed toward the Dolls

Just as the responses to clothes and houses by the Negro and white children involved quite different motivations by different children, so their expressed preferences for the dolls indicate the operation of several forces. The white doll is chosen as the "one liked best" by the percentages of children given in Table 5-XIII.

TABLE 5-XIII

	Kgn.	*1st*	*2nd*	*Total*
By Negro children	61%	59%	51%	57%
By white children	93%	84%	90%	89%

Note. Retest agreement is 82 percent by Negro children and 85 percent by white children.

Identification with the doll, feelings of racial prejudice, and awareness of cultural values which concede to white the "superior" status account for the majority of choices of the white children (see Table 5-XIV). Some of the responses in these categories are as follows (choices of white doll by white children):

> Him, because my whole family is white people.
> Because she's white. If a colored person came in, they would like the colored [doll] better.

> She's the same color as I am. I don't like colored, but that's all you can play with around here.
> I like white. I don't like no colored people, they're ashamed of themselves.

> 'Cause he's colored and carries knives.
> She is white; all people like white.
> 'Cause he has a cleaner job and a better job; 'cause he (Negro) is colored and has to work very hard; white doesn't.

TABLE XIV

REASONS FOR DOLL PREFERENCE
(Percentage of Children)

	Preferred Doll			
	Negro Doll		White Doll	
Reasons for Preference	*Negro Children*	*White Children*	*Negro Children*	*White Children*
Because of his race:				
"He's white," "not colored," "not nigger"	—	—	19	43
"He's Negro," "a colored man"	21	0	—	—
"I don't like colored," "I love white"	—	—	—	3
"I am like him"	3	—	—	8
"Colored man is better than white"	2	—	—	—
"White man is better than colored"	—	—	—	1
"Colored are bad (rob, beg, carry knives)"	—	—	—	3
Because of appearance:				
"He is prettier"	3	1	7	5
"He is clean, not dirty"	2	1	8	4
"He is dressed better"	6	4	10	14
Miscellaneous	6	5	13	8

The preferences of the Negro children are split almost evenly between white and Negro doll. The motivations are mixed. Identification with Negro doll is verbalized by only 3 percent of the Negro children (" 'Cause I'm colored"). A statement of preference because of race by 21 percent of the Negro children is usually just "Bcause he is colored"; occasionally, a stronger feeling is expressed ("Colored man is better than white man"). When the preference is given the white doll, it is explained by a racial preference by the Negro children (19 percent) thus: " 'Cause she has a white skin," "'Cause he is white." Most often preference for either doll is explained by the Negro children by referring to the appearance of clothes or to the "appearance" factors. Eleven percent prefer the Negro doll for these reasons, while 25 percent prefer the white doll for reasons of clothes or appearance which involve valuations disparaging to the Negro. These responses are illustrated below (choice of white doll by Negro children);

> He's the sweetest one.
> 'Cause he is clean.
> 'Cause she is lighter than the other.
> 'Cause she is the prettiest.

Thus, responses from the Negro children show not only their awareness of stereotypes imposed by the culture but also their acceptance of these stereotypes which undervalue their own race.

The question on friendship between the persons represented by the two dolls ("Do you think these two men are friends?") brought "yes" and "no" answers in about equal proportions (Table 5-XV). It is difficult to evaluate these responses, for a large part of the sample gave no reason for their response, and from that standpoint the question was ineffective. Twenty-five percent of the white children and 2 percent of the Negro children answered the "why" question. In their responses, one can see stereotypes, social status differences, and experiences linked with

TABLE 5-XV

	Negro Children	White Children
"Yes, they are friends"	63%	52%
"No, they are not friends"	36%	46%
No response	1%	2%

race translated into standards of behaving toward the other race. Thus, among the white children who say the dolls are friends and who give reasons, several cite such instances as "My father has colored friends." More frequently (4 percent), the friendship involves a special role for each person, thus: "Cleaning lady and neighbors are friends," "Colored works for white." The Negro children who say the men or women are friends never explain the friendship. White children who say the dolls are not friends refer in 13 percent of the cases to race as the barrier to friendship, as one race not liking the other. The full awareness of her family's feelings against Negroes is evidenced in the child's response: "No [they are not friends]. My father has to make friends with colored ladies when they come in the store."

Perception of Social-Racial Roles Compared with Attitudes toward Race

Descriptions of Negroes and whites in terms of inferior and superior social roles may or may not be diagnostic of the child's feelings toward either race. Whether perceptions of social inequalities are influenced by or influence feelings toward race at this early age is an important question from the standpoint of how a child's social philosophy is developed and what is necessary for the teaching of social democracy. With the data available it was possible to pursue this point as it relates to the reactions of the white children.

In another part of the research pictures were presented of Negro and white children on a playground and the children were asked to interpret the pictures and to answer questions about the pictures which probed their feelings toward each race. On the basis of these responses the children were classified as showing hostile feelings toward Negroes, as giving no evidence that "race" affected their reactions to the children in the pictures, or as indicating specifically friendly feelings toward Negroes. (The last two have been classified as "friendly" in the following comparisons.) The ratings on feelings toward Negroes were compared with the roles ascribed to Negroes. These comparisons show that not all white children who ascribe inferior social roles to Negroes express hostile feelings toward Negroes on the test of attitudes. Among the 38 percent who ascribe inferior roles to Negroes in costumes or houses, 81 percent are hostile or rejecting on the attitude test. The children who show no awareness of social distinctions in the costumes or houses express hostility on the attitude test in 60 percent of the cases. The percentages of the total white sample who express friendliness or hostility, with their corresponding responses on costumes and houses, are given in Table 5-XVI. The proportion of hostile children is lowest among the children whose costume or housing responses treat Negro and white dolls similarly, and highest where specific inferior roles or stereotypes are described.

There is, thus, a tendency for hostile feelings toward Negroes and a perception of Negroes in inferior roles to appear together; however, many children who show a dislike for Negroes show no awareness of the status factors studied. It remains for further research to determine how the two sets of data are related dynamically: whether experiences in which a Negro woman is known as a maid or a Negro family is known to live in a run-down house are generalized to characterize a whole race because of an already rejecting attitude toward Negroes, to which the experience only lends support for rejection or feelings of superiority; or whether the

TABLE 5-XVI

COMPARISON OF ATTITUDES EXPRESSED TOWARD NEGROES WITH
ROLES ASCRIBED TO NEGROES
(Responses of White Children in Percentages)

	Corresponding Attitude toward Negroes		Ratio of Friendly to Rejecting Children in Each Category of Role Description
	Friendly	Hostile	
Responses to costume:			
Similar activities or status for both dolls	23	31	1 : 1.4
Less pleasant activity or occupation ascribed to Negro doll	6	14	1 : 2.3
Inferior social role ascribed to Negro doll	5	21	1 : 4.2
Responses to houses:			
Equal house for both dolls, or better house for Negro doll	10	15	1 : 1.5
Poor house to Negro doll, good to white doll	16	32	1 : 2.0
Poor house to Negro doll with reason involving stereotype	5	22	1 : 4.4

experiences, first-hand and vicarious, give the materials out of which the child's avoidant feelings and behavior originate.

Most significant in the findings of this study is the fact that the prejudices of children (five to eight years of age) have within them extensive comprehension of social differentiations in which Negroes and whites are perceived and compared in a great variety of contexts and dimensions, and feelings and valuations of each race are bound up in these many sources. The problems for re-education of attitudes are thus problems of comprehension and motivation which must affect these many areas in the children's lives.

SUMMARY AND CONCLUSIONS

The purpose of the research was to study the perceptions of young children of the social roles of Negroes and whites in adult society. Two hundred and forty-two Negro and white children of kindergarten, first, and second grades were interviewed. Doll materials supplied stylized figures representing Negro and white adults, variations in costumes, and variations in houses. Assignments of costumes and houses to each doll and explanations of these assignments revealed the following data:

1. Although the materials of clothes and houses provided relatively small differences and no specific stereotypes of roles (maid, porter and the like), 38 percent of the white children introduced interpretations in which stereotyped and inferior social roles were ascribed to Negroes. This proportion is exclusive of the number of white children whose assignment of clothes or houses suggests status differences but whose explanations do not give specific verifying descriptions.

2. Among the Negro children, 16 percent ascribe inferior roles or circumstances to Negroes, mainly in relation to money and housing. This percentage for the Negro children is not presumed to indicate the number who are aware of social differences, for it is not expected that Negro children would express these stereotypes as freely as white children, since stereotypes involving status tend to be disparaging to the Negro race. Poor housing and clothes and low occupational status are undoubtedly unhappy issues for children in low socioeconomic homes regardless of race.

But these factors are more likely to be seen as existing *because of* their race by the Negro children than by the white children.

3. Expression of social status differences did not appear in the assignment of clothes. White and Negro children tended to dress-up the doll of their own race.

4. However, when describing what the dolls might be doing, 14 percent of the white children gave the Negro doll specific low-status roles, and 24 percent gave work to the Negro doll and leisure activities to the white doll.

The Negro children never verbalized specific low-status roles (maid, janitor) for the Negro doll; 8 percent gave work to the Negro doll while giving leisure to the white doll. Thirty-seven percent reversed the work and leisure roles, giving work to the white doll and leisure to the Negro doll. No specific socially advantaged roles were described for the white doll by the Negro children.

The threat which these social factors constitute for the Negro children, however, is evidenced sometimes in contradictory responses, sometime in avoidance, and sometimes in retaliatory statements.

5. In the selection of houses, the great majority of children from both races give the poor house to the Negro doll and the good house to the white doll. These assignments are accompanied by explanations which indicate that the child sees the race represented by the doll as "belonging" to that kind of house.

6. The test responses do not always correspond to what the child experiences in his immediate neighborhood. He responds, instead, in terms of cultural stereotypes and prejudices. This is particularly the case in reactions to the houses.

7. The white doll is the preferred doll by 89 percent of the white children. Their reasons for preference show feelings of identification with the race of the doll and feelings of prejudice against Negroes. The Negro children choose the Negro doll as the one they like best in only 57 percent of the cases. Few give reasons except to say "He is a Negro" or "a colored man." Those Negro children who prefer the white doll often mention factors of appearance or circumstance which express an undervaluing of their own race.

8. Inferior social roles are ascribed to Negroes by white children who express hostile attitudes toward Negroes and as well by children who express friendly attitudes toward Negroes on the attitude test. The inferior roles appear more frequently, however, among the children expressing hostile attitudes.

It must be repeated that the children responded freely, and that the atmosphere was completely permissive, with no urging or pressure by the interviewer and no indication that there was any "correct" or "right" answer. The concepts and attitudes toward race which the data of this study reveal seem to be formed from real and vicarious experiences which these children have had with the adult world. For the development of scientific concepts of race and democratic attitudes toward race, education cannot rely solely on congenial play relations among children, as many people assume. Play situations may be congenial and yet perceptions of Negroes and whites as a group may remain as role stereotypes and as inferior and superior.

The findings of this study emphasize the complex learning in young children's perceptions of race and reactions to race. For many of the children, concepts and feelings about race extend into adult-world distinctions of status, ability, character, occupations, and economic circumstances. Social distinctions made by whites which put Negroes in an inferior status tend to be accepted as "natural" or inevitable. For the Negro children these distinctions play an important role in self and group assessment as the factor of race appears inextricably related to many problem areas in life.

From the present data, it can be seen that part of the children's concepts of race include the factors of occupations, clothing, and housing. These factors become increasingly linked with race, and status quo group relations become justifications for discrimination.

The fact that the children's responses so clearly reflect the values of the adult culture has serious and urgent implications for education. If children are to make satisfactory adjustments to life situations, they must learn to recognize that group differences exist in their neighborhood and beyond. This learning of realities inevitably takes place in a context of democratic values that contradict many of the realities. Because of these very values, however, the contradiction can neither be ignored nor merely accepted, or the result will be an acceptance of the status quo, of social inequalities as somehow inherent accompaniments of group differences. Therefore, the experiences and learnings of young children must be consciously designed to develop attitudes compatible with good human relations.

Is such comprehension possible for five- to eight-year-old children? A controlled experiment involving 120 children in four schools was carried out in an attempt to cast light on this problem. The results of the experiment will be published shortly.

REFERENCE

1. RADKE, M., TRAGER, H., and DAVIS, H.: Social perceptions and attitudes of children. *Genet. Psychol. Monogr., 40,* 1949.

II. SOME MANIFESTATIONS OF PREJUDICE

Chapter 6

ARE JEWISH OR GENTILE CHILDREN MORE CLANNISH?

ADELINE HARRIS AND GOODWIN WATSON

Teachers College
Columbia University

T his study arose from an interest in discovering the importance of ethnic background (Jewish or non-Jewish) for children's choice of friends. Each of 82 children in grades IV to VI of an upper-class private school in New York City was asked to list the names of his best friends. No reference was made to race, religion, or any other basis of selection. First he was asked to choose his best friends from within his class, next his best friends from among all the children attending his school, finally his best friends among children he sees only outside of school. The average child supplied eight or nine nominations.

All the children in four classrooms were polled. They were equally divided between girls and boys. Approximately one third were Jewish; two thirds were Gentile. Ages ranged from eight to twelve.

It was often difficult to determine which of the children named were Jewish and which Gentile. Some of the teachers cooperating in the investigation were Jewish, others Gentile, and through their intimate knowledge of the families and community could contribute a great deal of information. In some cases it was necessary later to make discreet inquiries, usually from adults. It was thought important not to arouse in the minds of the children the idea that teachers attached any particular importance

Note. Reprinted by permission from *The Journal of Social Psychology*, 24:71-76, 1946.

to the Jewish-Gentile distinction. The results of the study are summarized in Table 6-I.

Within the class the choices of Jewish and Gentile children seem to be influenced by this difference in ethnic background. Each group chooses about one quarter of best friends from among the Jewish children and three quarters from among the Gentiles. Since the Gentiles constitute only two thirds of the class population, the Jewish children in this school apparently happen to be at a slight disadvantage in popularity, but this difference is less than twice its standard error and should not be overemphasized. The more striking fact is the absence of ingroup choices among Jewish children in this school. There is no more tendency for Jewish children to find their best classroom friends among Jews than there is for Gentile children to chooose Jewish friends in the same class. Apparently the classroom atmosphere is such that friends are chosen without reference to any such distinction.

The choice of friends outside of school is influenced more largely by parents, relatives, and neighbors. In this situation, the difference between Jewish and Gentile children is greater. As shown in Table 6-I each group has most of its friends from its own ingroup. The Gentiles, however, seem to be more "clannish" than the Jews. The Jewish children chose 28 percent of their out-of-school friends among non-Jews; the Gentile children chose only 6 percent of their out-of-school friends among Jews. This discrepancy is probably due in part to the fact that the total population of potential neighbors and friends is more largely Gentile. Whether or not this be the explanation, the finding is important. Jewish

TABLE 6-I

CHOICE OF BEST FRIENDS BY JEWISH AND GENTILE CHILDREN

	No. of Friends Mentioned	Proportion of Friends Who Are		
		Jewish	Gentile	Total
Gentiles (N = 56)				
Friends in class	174	22%	78%	100%
Friends in school	166	17%	83%	100%
Friends outside school	145	6%	94%	100%
Jewish (N = 26)				
Friends in class	78	24%	76%	100%
Friends in school	71	42%	58%	100%
Friends outside school	71	72%	28%	100%

children at this school are more likely to have friends outside their ethnic group than are the Gentile children.

The question about friends in the school but outside the child's own class falls midway between the other two questions. There is more tendency toward ingroup choice than we found when choices were limited to the immediate classroom and less than we found when choices were made from the home community. In the school we are dealing with a known population and can relate the choices to what would have resulted from a choice unrelated to Jewishness. A random sample of names in this age range in this school would have been 32 percent Jewish. The Gentile children, in choosing only 17 percent of their friends from among Jewish children, fell short of this actual proportion by 15 percent. Perhaps this may be taken as an approximate measure of their tendency to prefer non-Jews as friends. The Jewish children, in choosing 42 percent of their friends from among other Jews, exceeded the actual proportion in the school by 10 percent. Comparing 15 percent and 10 percent we may again conclude, and this time after due allowance for the available possible choices, that the Jewish children in this study show less tendency to be clannish and exclusive than do the Gentiles. A majority of the best school friends of the Jewish children are non-Jewish.

A breakdown of Table 6-I to show differences between girls and boys is presented in Table 6-II.

In choosing friends from their own class, both boys and girls choose mainly Gentile, agreeing with the pattern noted for the group as a whole. The slightly higher proportion of Jewish choices among the boys (both Gentile and Jewish) might perhaps be explained in part by the fact that children at this age usually choose friends of their own sex, and 37.5 percent of all the boys in these grades are Jewish while only 26 percent of the girls are Jewish.

This difference in available sample would not, however, affect the choice of friends outside of school. In every comparison, in school and out, the *Gentile girls* make a larger proportion of ingroup choices than do the Gentile boys. The sex roles are reversed in the Jewish population. The *Jewish boys* make more ingroup choices than do the Jewish girls. An interesting cultural hypothesis would be that greater efforts are made by Gentile homes to

TABLE 6-II

DIFFERENCES BETWEEN BOYS AND GIRLS IN CHOICE OF
JEWISH OR GENTILE FRIENDS

	No. of Friends Mentioned	Proportion of Friends Who Are		
		Jewish	Gentile	Total
Gentile boys (N = 25)				
Friends in class	75	27%	73%	100%
Friends in school	72	19%	81%	100%
Friends outside school	62	10%	90%	100%
Gentile girls (N = 31)				
Friends in class	99	18%	82%	100%
Friends in school	94	16%	84%	100%
Friends outside school	83	2%	98%	100%
Jewish boys (N = 15)				
Friends in class	45	29%	71%	100%
Friends in school	42	45%	55%	100%
Friends outside school	42	74%	26%	100%
Jewish girls (N = 11)				
Friends in class	33	18%	82%	100%
Friends in school	29	38%	62%	100%
Friends outside school	29	69%	31%	100%

"protect" girls; greater efforts by Jewish homes similarly to "protect" their boys. The numbers in this study are too small to give the observed differences satisfactory statistical reliability but their consistency suggests the desirability of a more extensive study.

Table 6-III gives a breakdown by classroom, and permits several interesting comparisons.

Two fourth grades participated. They are alike in size, ability, and social status, but IV-A contains 41 percent Jewish children while IV-B has 29 percent Jewish children. One not very surprising consequence, as shown in the first two columns of Table 6-III, is that a larger proportion of Jewish children are chosen as

TABLE 6-III

INGROUP CHOICES BY GRADE

	School Grade				
	IV-A	IV-B	V	VI	All
No. of pupils	22	21	21	18	82
Jewish pupils	41%	29%	29%	28%	32%
Gentile					
Classroom friends from ingroup	75%	83%	78%	77%	78%
Outside friends from ingroup	93%	98%	85%	100%	94%
Jewish					
Classroom friends from ingroup	34%	17%	28%	13%	24%
Outside friends from ingroup	72%	67%	84%	61%	72%

friends in the class where there are more to choose from. It is more surprising that this effect seems to be much more marked in the case of the Jewish children. In the IV-B class, with 29 percent of Jewish children, these Jewish children chose only 17 percent of their best friends from their own ethnic group. In the IV-A class, with 41 percent of Jewish children, they chose 34 percent from among their Jewish classmates. In neither case was the proportion of Jewish friends as high as would have been true if selection had been purely random. In IV-B, the Gentile children chose 17 percent of their best friends from among the Jews— exactly the same ratio as the choice made by Jewish children. In IV-A the Gentile children chose 25 percent of their best friends from among the Jewish children. Here again, in neither case is the proportion of Jewish friends as high as the proportion of Jewish classmates. An increase in the proportion of classmates who are Jewish results in an increased choice of school friends who are Jewish. In this instance the readiness of Gentile children to choose Jewish friends increased in about the same proportion as the increase in Jewish classmates. The readiness of Jewish children to choose Jewish friends increased, however, at more than twice the rate of their increase in the class population. This may be an accident of personalities in these two school grades or it may point to a subtle factor in intercultural group dynamics. The question deserves investigation in other classes and schools.

Does association with another group in school increase readiness to accept friends from that group outside of school? Our data cannot be conclusive, but they would support an affirmative answer. Gentile children in the fourth grade, which provided more Jewish classmates, chose 7 percent of their out-of-school friends from among the Jews, in the class with fewer Jewish associates, the out-of-school friends were only 2 percent Jewish. Jewish children in the predominantly Gentile class chose 33 percent of their out-of-school friends from among Gentiles; those from the class which provided fewer Gentile associates chose 28 percent of their friends from among Gentiles. Would a wider discrepancy in classroom proportions have been accompanied by still greater differences in outside associates? This, too, would be worth investigating.

The other comparison brought out in Table 6-III is relationship to maturity. Grades IV-B, V, and VI all have about the same proportion of Jewish children. It has commonly been observed that young children are relatively free from prejudice but that they acquire these conventional discriminations as they approach puberty. Within the narrow age range here represented (8-12) no such tendency appears. In three out of four comparisons the sixth graders made a smaller proportion of ingroup choices than did the pupils in lower grades, but differences are not consistent or statistically reliable.

The last column of Table 6-III affords a convenient summary of our findings on the basic question of this study. Table 6-III differs from earlier tables in that all data are here stated in terms of the ingroup choice. Outside of school, the Gentile children choose 94 percent of their friends from the ingroup, Jewish children only 72 percent. Within the classroom, the differences are far more striking. Gentile children showed 78 percent ingroup choices, Jewish children only 24 percent.

One other way of approaching the problem is to study those children who limit their choices exclusively to their ingroup. The data are shown in Table 6-IV. Among the Gentile children, 27 percent, or more than one in four, mentioned no Jewish child among the eight or nine friends he listed in his class, in the school, or outside school. Among the Jewish children there was none without some Gentile friends. Two boys listed Gentile friends exclusively.

TABLE 6-IV

CHILDREN LIMITING CHOICE OF FRIENDS TO THEIR INGROUP

	Total No. Pupils	No. Choosing 100% of Friends From Ingroup	Percent of Group
Gentile			
Boys	25	6	24%
Girls	31	9	29%
Total	56	15	27%
Jewish			
Boys	15*	0	0%
Girls	11	0	0%
Total	26	0	0%

*Two boys or 8 percent of the Jewish group chose all Gentile friends.

SUMMARY

A study of the choice of friends by 82 children in grades IV to VI of an upper-class private school in New York showed that Gentile children were less likely to choose Jewish friends than were Jewish children to choose Gentile friends. Ingroup choices were more characteristic of friends out of school than when choice was limited to classmates, but here also the Gentiles made more (94 percent) ingroup choices than did the Jews (72 percent). Gentile girls made more ingroup choices than did Gentile boys; among Jewish children the boys made more ingroup choices than did the girls. Probability that Jewish children will be chosen as school friends and as out-of-school friends increases as the proportion of Jewish children in the class rises. The effect is more marked on choices made by Jewish pupils than on those made by the Gentiles. No evidence was found of increase or decrease in exclusiveness from fourth to sixth grade. While one fourth of the Gentile children had no Jewish friends, all of the Jewish children had some Gentile friends.

Chapter 7

ETHNIC CLEAVAGE AMONG YOUNG CHILDREN

WALLACE E. LAMBERT AND YOSH TAGUCHI

McGill University

An apparent discrepancy exists between the age when preferential or prejudiced *attitudes* develop toward ethnically different people and the age when preferential or prejudiced *behavior* appears. A recent summary of research[6] places the appearance of prejudiced attitudes at the third or fourth years compared with the onset of prejudiced behavior at the eighth to tenth years. Moreno[11] found no sociometric evidence of behavioral cleavage among young children of various ethnic backgrounds until age ten (grade V). Criswell,[2] using the same technique, studied children from nursery school to the teen ages and found no cleavage until the eighth year (grade III). She noted that ethnic cleavage was most pronounced at the tenth year (grade V). The age determined by Moreno and Criswell is not only accepted as the established age of onset of prejudiced behavior in children, but their findings are also used as supporting evidence for theories of prejudice.[6] (p 1037)[6] (p 514)[8]

The appropriateness of Moreno's and Criswell's method is open to question. Standard sociometric questions are often not meaningful to preschool Ss. In preliminary work we found that four- and five-year-olds generally "liked everyone" and "didn't mind" who sat next to them, suggesting that young children may not discriminate favored associates on such issues. Discriminations may be made, however, if the more significant values of preschool children are incorporated in the choosing procedures. To test this possibility, we measured ethnic cleavage among young chil-

---

Note: Reprinted by permission.

dren with techniques which, we assume, are more meaningful to them.

METHOD

The thirteen *Ss* of this study comprised the total membership of a small nursery school in Montreal. Six children were of Japanese origin (Oriental) and seven were of Roumanian, Greek, German, and Polish ancestries (Occidental), but all thirteen spoke English fluently. They attended school from 9:00 A.M. to 5:00 P.M. five days a week since both parents of all the children normally worked in Montreal. The newest member had been in attendance for over two months when the investigation was begun. None of the children in the school lived close enough to one another to play together outside of school. Two of the Oriental and three of the Occidental *Ss* were male. The ages for Oriental *Ss* were 5.1, 5.6, 5.6, 5.8, 5.8, and 6.0; for the Occidental, 3.5, 4.0, 4.2, 5.5, 6.0, 6.0, and 6.2.

The experimenter (Taguchi, an Oriental) was introduced to the children as a guest supervisor (one regular supervisor was a white Canadian, the other an Oriental) and actively participated in the school program once each week for a month before the investigation commenced. All experimental work with the children began at 11:00 A.M. during the recreational period.

Types of Choices

Four-year-olds generally place high value on receiving or giving candy and on having their pictures taken. It was assumed that choices of associates would be meaningful to children if these values were made part of the choosing procedure. The *Ss* were asked (a) to give away a piece of candy to an associate and then receive one for themselves (candy-giving choices); (b) to choose an associate to pose with them for picture taking (picture-taking choices); and (c) to indicate which picture, from among individual poses of each school member, they liked best and would want to keep, excluding their own (picture-choosing choices). In each of these tests the child was taken individually to a side room and given directions for each situation. The candy-giving test was repeated twelve times during a four-week period while the other two tests occurred once only.

RESULTS AND DISCUSSION

The choices made in the three test situations are presented in Table 7-I. Exact tests of significance,[7] (p 303f) indicates a significant association between ethnic background and types of choices made, for all three situations. However, the tendency for Occidental children to choose within their own ethnic group is not a significant one since the probabilities of obtaining differences equal to or greater than a 4:3 and 5:2 split by chance alone are, respectively, 1.00 and .453 using an exact two-tailed test. Ethnic cleavage is clearly apparent, however, with the Oriental children. The Orientals' within-group preference is significant since the probabilities of obtaining a difference equal to or greater than a 6:0 split is .031 for each instance.

The findings indicate that ethnic cleavage appears among preschool children. We maintain that other researchers have not found prejudiced behavior at earlier ages because their methods of observation have not penetrated to the significant values of the younger Ss. Further research is clearly necessary in order to generalize this finding beyond Occidental-Oriental Ss and beyond so small and compact a group as that used here.

Davitz[3] has recently suggested that people have a basic need to be similar to valued persons, this need manifesting itself in a child's striving to be like his parents or an important peer. Davitz

TABLE 7-I

TEST CHOICES OF OCCIDENTAL AND ORIENTAL CHILDREN

	Candy-Giving Choices*		Picture-Taking Choices		Picture-Choosing Choices	
	In-group	Out-group	In-group	Out-group	In-group	Out-group
Occidentals	4	3	5	2	4	3
Orientals	6	0	6	0	6	0
Exact tests of significance	$p = .048$†		$p = .002$†		$p = .048$†	

*Mean choices for twelve repetitions of the procedure.
†Two-tailed tests of significance.

turns to Mowrer's theory of developmental identification[12] to account for such a need. For Mowrer, identification is equated with the secondary reward value of a person for the infant. Developmental identification starts with the interaction between the infant and the others in his social environment who satisfy his needs. When drive reduction and the cues associated with those who reduce the drives are repeatedly paired, the cues themselves take on secondary reward value for the infant. On a similarity gradient, schoolmates of the same ethnic background would be more like, at least in physical characteristics, the family members with whom the child has identified. Any secondary reward generated during the identification process would be more likely to generalize to like schoolmates.

It is apparent that Mowrer's theory accounts for the behavior of our Oriental *Ss* but does not explain the Occidental group's behavior. Our finding of "one-way" cleavage is not unique. Many researchers have noted the preferential choice of within-group members with school-age children. Criswell[2] noted that, when racial cleavage did appear, it was the Negro *Ss* who were the first to segregate themselves. Radke *et al.*[13] found that Jewish children, five to nine years old, were more emotionally identified with their own group than were Catholic or Protestant children. At the high school age, Loomis,[9] Goodnow and Taguiri,[5] and Lundberg[10] have all noted ethnic and religious within-group segregation.

It appears that minority group members (members of groups toward whom prejudice is commonly directed) are generally the first to segregate themselves from the majority group, this self-segregation occurring with preschool and young children as well as at the high school level. Mowrer's and Davitz's theories can be extended to account for this empirical fact. Nurturance needs arising in infancy are satisfied by people who have distinguishable cue properties. The cues, acting alone as secondary reward agents, may become more active agents whenever nurturance-type needs are activated. Minority status, with its aspects of threat, would regenerate similar needs and concomitantly intensify the significance and vividness of cues associated with own-group members. The secondary reward accompanying the cue properties of within-group associates will reduce the nurturance needs of minority group members in a mixed-group situation. Majority group members, with less environmental threats, will not experience increased nurturance-type needs in a mixed-group situation and will accordingly receive less reward from within-group situations.

Allport has discussed the self-segregation phenomenon in other terms. He believes that within-group cohesion mitigates the problems of minority group members by assuring them friendship,[1] (p 149) and permits them easier interaction where they need not learn new habits of social intercourse[1] (p 18).

A recent study by Goodman,[4] however, poses problems for both Mowrer and Allport, and suggests that further attention should be given to prejudiced behavior among young children. Goodman found that Negro preschool children often showed preference for *white* characters in stories, white dolls, and even white people.

SUMMARY

Ethnic cleavage among preschool children was studied using various test situations where choices of associates could be observed. It was found that ethnic cleavage does exist when choices are made significant to young children. The results are compared with other related findings and attempts are made to explain them theoretically.

REFERENCES

1. ALLPORT, G. W.: *The Nature of Prejudice.* Cambridge, Mass., Addison-Wesley, 1954.
2. CRISWELL, JOAN H.: Racial cleavage in Negro-white groups. *Sociometry, 1*:85-89, 1937.
3. DAVITZ, J. R.: Social perception and sociometric choice of children. *J. Abnorm. Soc. Psychol., 50*:173-176, 1955.
4. GOODMAN, MARY ELLEN: *Race Awareness in Young Children.* Cambridge, Mass., Addison-Wesley, 1952.
5. GOODNOW, R. E., and TAGIURI, R.: Religious ethnocentrism and its recognition among adolescent boys. *J. Abnorm. Soc. Psychol., 47*:316-320, 1952.
6. HARDING, J., KUTNER, B., PROSHANSKY, H., and CHEIN, I.: Prejudice and ethnic relations. In G. Lindzey (Ed.): *Handbook of Social Psychology.* Cambridge, Mass., Addison-Wesley, 1954, Ch. 27.

7. KENDALL, M. G.: *The Advanced Theory of Statistics.* London, Griffin, 1943.
8. KLINEBERG, O.: *Social Psychology.* New York, Holt, 1954.
9. LOOMIS, C. P.: Ethnic cleavages in the southwest as reflected in two high schools. *Sociometry, 6*:7-26, 1943.
10. LUNDBERG, A., and DICKSON, L.: Selective association among ethnic groups in a high school population. *Amer. Sociol. Rev., 17*:23-34, 1952.
11. MORENO, J. L.: *Who Shall Survive?* Washington, Nervous and Mental Disease Pub. Co., 1934.
12. MOWRER, O. H.: *Learning Theory and Personality Dynamics.* New York, Ronald, 1950.
13. RADKE, M., TRAGER, H. G., and DAVIS, H.: Social perceptions and attitudes of children. *Genet. Psychol. Monogr., 40*:327-347, 1949.

Chapter 8

SEX, ETHNICITY, AND PLAY PREFERENCES OF PRESCHOOL CHILDREN

Boyd R. McCandless and June M. Hoyt

Iowa Child Welfare Research Station

In the literature concerned with ethnocentrism, few studies have been concerned with preschool-age children. Moreno[4] and Criswell,[1] using sociometric techniques, found no evidence of ethnocentric cleavage until about eight to ten years of age. Lambert and Taguchi[3] suggest that such cleavage exists in preschool children, but is not demonstrated in the kinds of choice required by the standard sociometric techniques. They devised choices that they assumed were more meaningful to young children, and found that their measure elicited ethnocentric choices in Oriental children in a Montreal preschool, but that the comparable trend among Occidental children was not statistically significant. Among possible explanations, the authors considered that the Oriental children, as a minority group, perceive more threat in a mixed racial situation than do the Occidentals, and hence cling more closely together.

In an intensive study of race awareness in Negro and white children of preschool age, Goodman[2] found that cross-racial interactions of children did not differ in frequency from that which would be expected by chance, although interactions of white with

Note. Reprinted by permission from *The Journal of Abnormal and Social Psychology,* 62 (3):683-685, 1961.

The authors are particularly indebted to Hannah Lou Bennett and Carolyn B. Bilous for providing the opportunity to conduct this study, to Betty Crooker and Mary Rushit for opening their preschool groups to the senior author, and to Mark Beals for his help in establishing reliability of observations. The basic data were collected while the senior author was a Carnegie Visiting Professor at the University of Hawaii.

white were 8 percent below chance, while those of Negro with Negro were 9 percent above chance. Goodman[2] (p 259) concludes:

> The high rate of Negro-Negro interaction and the low rate of white-white interaction must therefore result from the operation of variables of a nonracial order. We conclude that these variables are personality traits which are unequally distributed between the Negro and the white children in this particular group.

In the present study it was hypothesized that, in a situation where social mixing of races is common, preschool children show little tendency toward ethnic cleavage. Choice of play companions in a free play situation was assumed to be an interaction, meaningful to the child, in which this hypothesis could be tested.

METHOD

Subjects were 33 children of Oriental (non-*haole*) ethnic origin and 26 Caucasian (*haole*) children at the University of Hawaii preschools. The age range was from three years, six months to five years, three months, with a mean age of four years, five months. All except one child had been in the preschools for at least six months, this exception being the senior author's youngest child, who was a newcomer to her group. There were 17 boys and 16 girls in the non-*haole* group and 11 boys and 15 girls in the *haole* group. Three subjects were eliminated: one girl because she did not fall into either of the ethnic groups under study, one blind child who did not socialize with anyone, and one mentally defective boy.

The children were observed in free play in their regular preschool groups, the ethnic and sex composition of the three groups being approximately the same. The time-sampling method employed in making observations consisted of 15 five-minute observations for each child, during which time the duration and type of his interactions with other children were recorded. Three observers studied the children over a period of approximately three and a half months. Percentage of exact agreement for Observers A and B was 92; and for A and C, 93. A tabulation was made of total time spent with every child with whom the child under observation interacted during the observation periods, and total time was computed for interactions with children in each of the two ethnic groups.

The chance expectancy for time spent playing with *haole* and non-*haole* children was computed for each preschool group on the basis of the ethnic proportion in the group. For example, if a group is made up of 11 *haole* children and ten non-*haole* children, the chance expectancy for a given *haole* child for each ethnic group is 50 percent of his time. If he spent a total of 60 minutes in free play, it would be exxpected that 30 of these were spent with other *haole* children and 30 with non-*haole* children. From this base, discrepancy scores were computed. For our hypothetical *haole* child, if he spent 45 minutes playing with other *haoles,* the discrepancy score would be $+15$. The same procedure was used to study free play as related to sex.

Comparisons were made, using a chi-square analysis, of non-*haole* and *haole* children's choices of play companions based on this discrepancy score. The mean discrepancy was determined for each ethnic group, and separate comparisons were made within each group by sex of child. Comparable analyses were made for choice of companion by sex without regard to ethnic group.

RESULTS

The chi-square analysis, Yates' correction, demonstrates that, disregarding ethnic group, boys overchoose boys as play companions, and girls overchoose girls ($_x^2 = 32.9$; for $p = .01$, 1 df, 6.635 required). There was also an ethnic cleavage in choice of play companion ($_x^2$ for 1 $df = 6.9$). In other words, boys played more with boys, girls with girls, disregarding ethnic group; and, disregarding sex, *haoles* played more with *haoles,* non-*haoles* with non-*haoles.*

Table 8-I summarizes the distribution of play times by subgroups, and Table 8-II shows the mean time beyond chance expectancies associated with these choices. The sex cleavage was significantly more extreme for boys than girls, although both spent more than the expected proportion of their time playing with children of their own sex. The ethnic cleavages did not differ significantly for the *haole* and non-*haole* children, contrary

TABLE 8-I

MEAN TIME AND STANDARD DEVIATIONS IN MINUTES SPENT
AND PREDICTED BY CHANCE BY DESIGNATED GROUPS
IN PLAY WITH EACH OTHER

	Actual Time		Chance Expectancy Time	
	M	SD	M	SD
Boys with boys	114.6	42.9	72.9	22.8
Boys with girls	46.4	30.1	88.1	23.1
Girls with boys	42.8	27.2	63.3	28.8
Girls with girls	82.7	33.8	62.1	25.0
Orientals (non-*haole*) with non-*haole*	91.1	49.6	78.6	34.6
Non-*haole* with Caucasian (*haole*)	53.8	24.7	66.2	26.3
Haole with *haole*	63.4	26.6	56.8	15.6
Haole with non-*haole*	75.7	39.2	82.3	27.7

to the finding of Lambert and Taguchi,[3] nor did boys differ from
girls in this respect.

DISCUSSION

Contrary to hypothesis, it was found that children in this study
differentially selected play companions of their own ethnic group,
even in an atmosphere that, subjectively, would be presumed to

TABLE 8-II

MEAN TIME IN MINUTES BEYOND CHANCE EXPECTANCY SPENT
IN OBSERVED PLAY WITH COMPANIONS INDICATED

Play Companions	Mean Excess Over Chance	SD	t
Without regard to ethnic group:			
Boys playing with boys	41.7	29.3	
Girls playing with girls	20.5	15.9	
Total difference from expectancy (boys plus girls)	30.6	25.5	10.10*
Difference between boys and girls	21.2		3.44*
Without regard to sex:			
Non-*haoles* playing with non-*haoles*	12.4	24.5	
Haoles playing with *haoles*	6.6	25.3	
Total difference from expectancy (boys plus girls)	9.2	25.11	2.87*
Difference between non-*haoles* and *haoles*	5.8		.88
Ethnic group by sex:			
Non-*haoles* playing with non-*haoles*			
Boys	15.4	28.3	
Girls	9.3	18.3	
Difference	6.1		.70
Haoles playing with *haoles*			
Boys	11.9	33.2	
Girls	2.7	16.3	
Difference	9.2		.88

* $p = <.01$ for 57 $df.$

be more accepting of interracial companionships than might be expected in the Montreal setting of the Lambert and Taguchi[3] study.

The statistical analysis revealed a trend that had not been suggested to the senior author as he gathered the rather intensive observational material for the children. At no time did he hear an instance of verbal rejection that included ethnic reference, and his subjective judgment was that friendships and play contacts were the usual functions, found in ethnically more homogeneous preschool groups, of personality attributes, play interests, sex, and accident. In other words, he would have predicted the sex difference, but not the ethnic difference.

The authors consider that prejudice is based on hostility, and, for this reason, tentatively suggest that the ethnic "discriminaton" found among these children is not prejudice as usually thought of, but some sort of "comfort" differential by ethnic group. Ethnically different background, in the sense of such factors as greater commonality of food habits within the ethnic group, colloquialisms drawn from the original parent language (such as the terms used for toileting), perhaps subtly different play experiences and interests may operate to make the *haole* youngster feel more comfortable with other *haoles* (he has "more in common with them"). Similar factors may operate for the non-*haoles*. In other words, children in one ethnic group do not actively *avoid* members of the other group, but differentially *approach* the members of their own group.

Informal checking over the families and their patterns of out-of-school social interaction indicated that neither the non-*haole* nor *haole* parents in this Honolulu metropolitan area associated selectively with each other (i.e. the *haole* parents knew the non-*haole* parents as well as they did the *haole*, and did not appear to have selective out-of-school association with them by ethnic group, and vice versa). It is possible, however, even in cosmopolitan Honolulu, that, overall, the out-of-school play and visting contacts of non-*haole* youngsters are more frequently with other non-*haoles*, and likewise for the *haole* children. This probably contributes to the "comfort" or "compatibility" factor previously mentioned.

SUMMARY

Preschool children of Oriental (non-*haole*) and Caucasian (*haole*) background were observed, using a time-sampling technique, and their choices of play companions were analyzed. Children in both ethnic groups were found to prefer play companions of their own sex, this tendency being more pronounced in boys than in girls. *Haole* children spent more of their time with *haole* children and non-*haole* children with non-*haole* children than would be predicted on the basis of proportional representation of each of the two groups. The subjective impressions of the senior author were that this cleavage was not due to prejudice in any conventional sense, but possibly to differential "comfort" due to more common backgrounds among the members of a given ethnic group.

REFERENCES

1. CRISWELL, JOAN H.: Racial cleavage in Negro-white groups. *Sociometry, 1*:85-89, 1937.
2. GOODMAN, MARY E.: *Race Awareness in Young Children.* Cambridge, Mass., Addison-Wesley, 1952.
3. LAMBERT, W. E., and TAGUCHI, YOSH.: Ethnic cleavage among young children. *J. Abnorm. Soc. Psychol., 53*:380-382, 1956.
4. MORENO, J. L.: *Who Shall Survive?* Washington, Nervous and Mental Disease Pub. Co., 1934.

Chapter 9

SELECTIVE ASSOCIATION AMONG ETHNIC GROUPS IN A HIGH SCHOOL POPULATION

GEORGE A. LUNDBERG AND LENORE DICKSON

University of Washington

This paper reports (a) the extent to which students in a large American high school choose associates for four different types of social relationships (1) from their own ethnic group and (2) from other ethnic groups, (b) the relative popularity of the different ethnic groups as reflected in the choices of members of each group, and (c) the association of certain factors (sex, school class, age, membership in organizations, and socioeconomic status) with the number and kind of choices made.

POPULATION

This particular high school was selected for analysis because it draws its students not only from the crowded "skidroad" district, but also from some of the wealthiest and most "restricted" neighborhoods of the city. At the time of the study, the total enrollment was 1544 students, 1360 of whom filled in questionnaires. This represents 88 percent of the total enrollment who were present in school on May 27, 1948. The 12 percent not returning questionnaires represent the usual number of absentees on any given day, plus one of those present whose schedule was too defective to be included.

Note. Reprinted by permission from *American Sociological Review,* 17:23-24, 1952. The authors are indebted to Dr. Paul Neurath and Dr. S. C. Dodd for valuable criticisms of the original draft of this report. Since not all of their suggestions have been incorporated, these critics are in no sense responsible for the faults that remain. We acknowledge also financial assistance from the University of Washington Research Committee for machine tabulation of some of the data.

The ethnic background of the majority of the students was non-Jewish white (59.6 percent), while 15.9 percent were Jewish, 9.6 percent Japanese, 8.5 percent Negro, 4.8 percent Chinese, and 1.6 percent "other" (Filipino, Hawaiian, and Indian).[1] The non-Jewish whites were nearly all descended from northwestern Europeans. The parents of 32.7 percent of the students were managers, owners, or professional workers. The students ranged in age from 13 to 20, and except for a very small freshman class (4.6 percent), were equally distributed by school classes. The two sexes were equally represented. Nearly one third of the students held part-time jobs and nearly two thirds planned to attend college. About half the students belonged (or had belonged) to school organizations, and 21.5 percent held (or had held) school offices. One fifth belonged to the scholastic honor society. Ten percent were Roman Catholic, 43 percent Protestant, 16 percent Jewish, and 3 percent "other" (mostly Buddhist), while 28 percent attended no church. The non-Jewish white majority did not differ markedly from the minorities, taken as a whole, in any of these respects except religion.[2]

METHOD

The principal data were secured through a questionnaire which, in addition to the usual questions regarding the student's personal characteristics, school class, membership in organizations, socioeconomic status, and plans after completing high school, called for the following information:

1. Name three students whom you would like to have represent your high school next week at a big national meeting of high school students.

---

[1]"Ethnic" is used throughout this study to include racial and religious classifications as regards the six groups here selected for analysis. "Jewish" was defined as any person who (a) checked "Jewish" in the list of ethnic backgrounds, (b) answered affirmatively the question regarding Jewish church attendance, or (c) belonged to an organization avowedly Jewish.

[2]More detailed figures on the composition of the population may be found in Lenore Dickson, *Social Distance in Two Seattle High Schools*, M.A. thesis, unpublished, University of Washington Library, 1951. The religious classification was made on the basis of answers to the question "If you go to church, which church?"

2. If all the students were asked to help on a school picnic, which three students would you like to work with?

3. If you could have a *date* with *anyone in this school*, which three people would you choose?

4. Who are your three best friends in this high school (boys or girls)?[3]

The questionnaires were administered by the teachers, after an explanatory statement, during first-period classes. No attempt was made to give the questionnaire to absentees. However, school officials gave us their file of advisor's cards which gave most of the data (other than answers to the choice questions) for the absent individuals.[4]

The first general objective was to answer the question: What is the relative degree of ethnocentrism of the different ethnic groups with respect to choosing leaders, work partners, dates, and

---

[3]This was followed by a fifth question: "If you think any of the students you listed in question 4 will choose you as one of their best friends, place an X in front of their names." The results of this question are not included in the present paper but will appear in a subsequent article which will also report the results of a question regarding negative choices, i.e. people *disliked*. See G. Lundberg and L. Dickson, "Further Observations of Interethnic Relations in a High School Population," *American Journal of Sociology*, May, 1952.

[4]Since choices might include anyone enrolled, regardless of whether he was present or absent on the day of the study, the percentages and computations in subsequent tables are based on the full enrollment (1544) rather than on the 88 percent who completed questionnaires. A comparison of the personal characteristics of absentees (information supplied by school records) with similar characteristics of students in attendance revealed that the absentees differed to a statistically significant degree (at the 0.01 level) from students present on the day the questionnaire was given in the following respects: The absentees were charactrized by a higher proportion of (a) non-Jewish whites and Chinese, (b) males, (c) scholastic honor society, and (d) persons whose parents were not owners, managers, or professional workers. The fact that older students, but not those farther along in school, were more likely to be absent, seems to indicate that being older than one's classmates is a contrlbuting factor toward absenteeism. On the basis of our findings on factors associated with ethnocentrism, we should predict that absentees—especially the non-Jewish whites—are less ethnocentric than the average high school student. On the basis of our study at another high school on factors making for unpopularity, it appears that the unpopularity of absentees is due, in part, to certain of their personal and social characteristics. In view of the fact that our sample included 88 percent of the total population, the results given below could not, of course, be biased by more than 12 percent in any of the respects given above. (Actually, about one third of the "absentees" had dropped out of school, so that only about 8 percent were absent in the usual sense.)

best friends? To answer this question the number of choices which each ethnic group gave (a) to itself and (b) to each other group on each of the four questions were tabulated. The Criswell self-preference index[5] was then computed for each ethnic group on each of these questions. The word "ethnocentrism" in this paper is defined entirely in terms of the Criswell index.

A second general question which the study undertook to answer was the following: What characteristics are associated with choosing members of outgroups, and what characteristics are associated with ethnocentrism? Since the comparatively small number of members of the different minorities permitted a more intensive analysis of their characteristics,[6] only the data for non-Jewish whites were subjected to machine tabulation. For each non-Jewish white an IBM card was punched giving his background characteristics, and, for each question, whether he chose (a) no one, (b) only other non-Jewish whites, or (c) one or more outgroup persons. Then cross-tabulations were made for each question for each background characteristic according to whether the individual made an outgroup choice or not. The hypothesis of no association was then tested for each table by the chi-square technique using the .05 critical level.

For the minority groups the technique used was similar enough

---

[5]Joan H. Criswell, "Sociometric Methods in Measuring Group Preferences," *Sociometry*, 6:398-408, November, 1943. This index interprets the actual distribution of choices in relation to the distribution which would occur by chance. This is a double ratio given by the formula shown below. This index varies from zero to infinity. A value of one indicates that the ingroup has no preference one way or another between itself and the outgroup. A value of less than one indicates that the outgroup is preferred, and a value greater than one indicates self-preference or ethnocentrism. For a detailed discussion of the mathematical and logical implications of the Criswell index, see Paul Lazarsfeld, "Some Notes on the Use of Indices in Social Research," mimeographed, 24 pp., Department of Sociology, University of Washington, Seattle, 1948. "If there were few outgroup choices, one more or less makes much difference. If there are already many, the index plays down the adding or subtracting of one more."

[6]Reported in the following M.A. theses, University of Washington Library: Marilyn Graalfs, *A Sociometric Study of Chinese Students in a Polyethnic High School*; Virginia Hertzler, *A Sociometric Study of Japanese Students in a Polyethnic High School*; Jessie Reichel, *A Sociometric Study of Jewish Students in a Polyethnic High School*.

to allow a comparison.[7] Each choice was classified according to whether it was given to the ingroup or to the outgroup (i.e. other groups taken as a whole). Then, as for the majority group, the hypothesis that there was no association between each characteristic and outgroup choosing was tested by the chi-square technique, again using the .05 level of significance.

As will appear below, the data when analyzed yield answers to a very large number of specific questions in addition to the general questions discussed above. Examination of the principal questions of choice will show that the first three questions pose hypothetical situations, whereas the fourth question asks for information about an actually existing situation. Also, the relationships of leadership, work-partnership, dating, and friendship were selected on the hypothesis that each of their relationships arouse different degrees of ingroup and outgroup attitudes. That is, we were interested to discover whether and to what extent (a) ingroup attitudes vary according to the relationship specified and (b) whether the order variation is the same for all groups. For example, do all groups show highest ethnocentrism on dating and lowest on choice of leaders? What is the social distance (as measured by the Criswell index) of each group to every other group in each of the four relationships into which inquiry was made? Numerous other questions to which the data yield answers will be specified as they arise.

DATA AND DISCUSSION

Frequency and overlapping of choices. The students answering the questionnaire chose 3489 friends, 3432 leaders, 3199 work partners, and 2352 dates.[8]

---

[7]In the case of the minorities, (on account of their relatively small numbers) *choices* rather than *choosers* were classified according to the same classifications as were employed in the majority group. This might result in slightly exaggerating the figures of outgroup choices on the part of minorities as compared with the method used for the majority.

[8]The relatively low number of choices of dates is probably attributable to several considerations: (1) The younger group has not yet become involved in this relationship. (2) A number of students indicated they preferred dating with people outside of high school. (3) A number of students indicated loyalty to only one date

Some evidence of the degree to which each of the four questions did, in fact, tap different areas or degrees of sociability may be found in the extent to which students chose the same or different persons on each question. The frequency with which the same person was picked on each pair of questions was as follows:

1. Work-Friendship 1010
2. Work-Leadership 632
3. Leadership-Friendship 374
4. Work-Dating 259
5. Leadership-Dating 232
6. Dating-Friendship 143

By far the most popular combination was Work-Friendship, which is followed in frequency by Work-Leadership. It may be that students have two criteria in mind when choosing persons with whom to work, namely, (a) someone they like—a friend, and (b) someone who will get the work done. The latter may also be a principal quality desired in a leader, hence the high duplication of choices for work partners and leaders. On the other hand, only comparatively infrequently do students appear to feel that the person desired for leadership must be also their friend, and even less frequently do they feel that they would care to date with the person they have chosen for leadership. Likewise, they apparently find that the sentimental aspect of dating is not compatible with the best work relationship. Least of all do they find the same person in the role of both friend and date.[9]

Out of the 10,139 total choices made, there were (a) 8120 cases in which the individual was chosen on only one question by the same chooser. This indicates that the questions used were rather effective in distinguishing different roles and the extent

---

by refusing to name more than one choice on this question. (4) The dating question was regarded as more personal than the rest and was admittedly more frequently not answered for this reason. Also, since dates are limited to the opposite sex, there is a smaller total to choose from.

[9]From one point of view, dating might be expected to represent a *preferred* friend. However, the data indicate that this is not necessarily so among high school students of the type included in this study. There is reason to believe that the words "date" and "friend" represent to these high school students, at least, rather exclusive categories of different types. For example, friends are chosen predominantly from among persons of the same sex; dates are, by definition, of the other sex.

to which different persons are thought of as best fulfilling different roles. (b) In 1724 cases the same individual was chosen on two questions by the same person; (c) in 280 cases the same individual was chosen on three questions by the same person; and (d) in only 15 cases was the same individual chosen on all four questions by the same person. The most common three-question combination was leadership-work-friendship; 194 such cases occurred.

The choices of the different ethnic groups on each of the four questions. The general index of self-preference for each of the ethnic groups (as against all outsiders taken together) on each question is given in Table 9-I. Every ethnic group showed a preference for its own members in each of the four relationships covered by the questions (i.e. all the indices are more than 1.0).

We find the lowest ethnocentrism is shown by Jews in choosing leaders, and the greatest by Negroes in choosing friends. It may be that Jews, being relatively popular with the rest of the school, are friendly in return, while Negroes, who were very infrequently chosen as friends by the other groups, retaliated by making few outgroup choices of friends. If so, however, the Negroes appear to have overcompensated in their retaliation because they were conspicuously *more* disposed to avoid choosing friends among other groups than these other groups avoided choosing Negroes as friends, as will appear below. (But see footnote 11 for an important qualification of the conclusions from Table I.)

The rank of each ethnic group with respect to their ethnocentrism on each of the four questions is shown in Table 9-II. We find that Jews are relatively nonethnocentric on all questions, and Negroes relatively ethnocentric. The relative position of the other groups varied from questions to question—especially that of the

TABLE 9-I

GENERAL (CRISWELL) INDEX OF SELF-PREFERENCE FOR EACH
ETHNIC GROUP ON EACH QUESTION

Ethnic Group	Leadership	Work	Dating	Friendship
Non-Jewish white	8.5	8.5	14.7	6.3
Chinese	3.2	12.2	34.1	47.8
Japanese	2.7	6.2	12.2	53.2
Jewish	1.2	3.6	3.7	16.7
Negro	7.4	10.6	22.4	66.4

TABLE 9-II

ETHNIC GROUPS RANKED FROM HIGH TO LOW
ETHNOCENTRISM ON EACH QUESTION

Leadership	Work	Dating	Friendship
Non-Jewish white	Chinese	Chinese	Negro
Negro	Negro	Negro	Japanese
Chinese	Non-Jewish white	Non-Jewish white	Chinese
Japanese	Japanese	Japanese	Jewish
Jewish	Jewish	Jewish	Non-Jewish white

non-Jewish whites, who were the most ethnocentric group in choosing leaders but the least ethnocentric in choosing friends.

Relative friendliness among the ethnic groups is shown in Table 9-III. For each ethnic group on each question the four outgroups ranked from most liked to least liked, as indicated by the self-preference indices given in parentheses. For example, on leadership the ethnocentrism index of the non-Jewish whites with respect to Chinese was 18.7; with respect to Japanese, 25.3; with respect to Jews, 6.0; and with respect to Negroes, 6.5. Therefore, we can say that non-Jewish whites like Jews best (or dislike them least), Negroes second, Chinese third, and Japaneses least.

Non-Jewish whites were the most chosen group on leadership, work, and dating, but were chosen only moderately frequently on friendship. Negroes were second highest in choices of leaders but very little chosen on the other three questions. Japanese were also disliked—by all groups on leadership, and by all but the Chinese on other questions.

Non-Jewish whites and Jews liked each other best (next to themselves) on all questions. Japaneses liked Chinese best (next to themselves) as friends and second only to non-Jewish whites on the other questions, while Chinese liked Japanese best (next to themselves) as friends and dates, second best as work partners, and less than any other outgroup as leaders. Racial similarity would seem to account for these friendships. Less easy to explain is the marked antipathy which Japanese and Jews showed each other on all questions; perhaps the fact that both groups value scholastic success and also that they are the two largest minority groups in school make for competition.

The most interesting of the interethnic relations were those

TABLE 9-III

RELATIVE FRIENDLINESS AMONG ETHNIC GROUPS IN CHOOSING LEADERS, WORK PARTNERS, DATES, AND FRIENDS

Ranking from Most Liked to Least Liked of Each Group by Group in Stub of Table
(In Terms of Criswell Index)

Ethnic Group of Choosers	Most Liked	Second Most Liked	Third Most Liked	Least Liked
Leadership				
Non-Jewish white	Jewish (6.0)	Negro (6.5)	Chinese (18.7)	Japanese (25.3)
Chinese	Non-Jewish white (2.4)	Negro (6.0)	Jewish (9.6)	Japanese (20.5)
Japanese	Non-Jewish white (2.0)	Chinese (4.4)	Negro (4.5)	Jewish (16.8)
Jewish	Non-Jewish white (0.9)	Negro (5.3)	Chinese (8.9)	Japanese (24.0)
Negro	Non-Jewish white (5.3)	Jewish (26.0)	Chinese (27.3)	Japanese (36.9)
Work				
Non-Jewish white	Jewish (5.9)	Chinese (9.5)	Negro (13.4)	Japanese (18.1)
Chinese	Non-Jewish white (9.5)	Japanese (12.3)	Jewish (40.5)	Negro (87.0)
Japanese	Non-Jewish white (4.9)	Chinese (5.3)	Jewish (14.9)	Negro (34.7)
Jewish	Non-Jewish white (2.7)	Negro (13.4)	Chinese (16.9)	Japanese (84.2)
Negro	Non-Jewish white (7.7)	Jewish (31.1)	Chinese (65.3)	Japanese (66.2)
Dating				
Non-Jewish white	Jewish (6.9)	Chinese (22.9)	Negro (102.6)	Japanese (116.2)
Chinese	Japaneses (25.3)	Non-Jewish white (27.7)	Jewish (62.4)	Negro*
Japanese	Non-Jewish white (9.0)	Chinese (9.3)	Jewish (62.0)	Negro*
Jewish	Non-Jewish white (2.6)	Chinese (27.0)	Japanese-Negro*	Negro-Japanese*
Negro	Non-Jewish white (15.4)	Jewish (112.4)	Japanese (136.9)	Chinese*
Friendship				
Non-Jewish white	Jewish (4.3)	Chinese (6.4)	Japanese (11.6)	Negro (12.6)
Chinese	Japanese (33.9)	Jewish (55.7)	Non-Jewish white (57.2)	Negro (179.5)
Japanese	Chinese (22.8)	Non-Jewish white (57.4)	Jewish (76.1)	Negro (81.8)
Jewish	Non-Jewish white (13.5)	Chinese (23.5)	Japanese (57.2)	Negro (126.3)
Negro	Non-Jewish white (61.0)	Jewish (72.8)	Chinese (131.2)	Japanese (132.9)

Note. Table reads: For leadership non-Jewish whites prefer, among the minority groups, Jews first, Negroes second, Chinese third, and Japanese least.

*The asterisk indicates that no choices at all were given to that group by the group in stub of table (i.e. the index is infinity).

between the non-Jewish whites and each of the minorities.[10] Table
9-III shows that in choosing leaders, work-partners, and dates, non-
Jewish whites showed more prejudice toward Japanese, Jews, and
Negroes than these minorities showed toward them. But in choosing friends, non-Jewish white prejudice toward the minorities
was less than that of the prejudice of the minorities toward the
non-Jewish white. (Non-Jewish white prejudice toward Chinese
was greater than Chinese prejudice toward non-Jewish white on
leadership, equal on work, and less on dating and friendship.)

One possible interpretation of this finding is that the minorities desire more contact with the majority group than is desired
in return (as evidenced by the minorities' lower self-preference
on the first three [hypothetical] questions); but in the actual situation—friendship—they do not choose from the majority group
as frequently (relatively) as the majority choose from the minorities. This may be due to overcompensation for rebuffs received
when making overtures to the majority *in other relations*. Extreme ethnocentrism on the part of minorities in the choice of
friends may be a sort of defense mechanism from the ethnocentrism of other groups *in other relationships*.

As regards the choices by specific ethnic groups of members
of other ethnic groups, in only a single case did members of an
ethnic group prefer a specific outgroup to themselves, and then
only on the leadership question. This was the case of Jews indicating a small degree of preference (Criswell Index .9, Table
9-III) for non-Jewish whites as leaders. All other minority groups
chose leaders most frequently from the non-Jewish whites, next
to their own group. Non-Jewish whites chose leaders from among
the Jews most frequently, next to themselves. The Japanese were

---

[10]Of the 786 non-Jewish whites who filled in questionnaires, 466, or 59.3 percent,
did not choose even one minority person on any of the four questions. Since non-
Jewish whites constitute 59 percent of the school enrollment, the probability of one
choice going to a non-Jewish white is .59 if chance alone were operating. But the
students made an average of 9.2 choices. Therefore, the chance probability of one
student choosing only non-Jewish whites is $(.59)^{9.2}$ or .0039. Multiplying by 786 (the
number of non-Jewish whites who filled out quetsionnaires) we find that by chance
only 3.07 (rather than 466) would have made no outgroup choices. The difference
between three and 466 represents in a sense a measure of the "consciousness of kind"
among the non-Jewish whites.

proportionally least chosen as leaders by all the groups, perhaps in part because they had been away in relocation centers until three years before the time of the study and in the length of time since their return had not been able to establish themselves in the political life of the school. Every group ranked the Negroes second or third in preference rank in their choice of leaders. These results may be explained, at least in part, by the fact that there were in the school two exceptionally popular Negro boys prominent in school activities.

Comparison of ingroup and outgroup choosing on the four questions. All minority groups were least ethnocentric in choosing leaders, but became progressively ethnocentric in choosing work partners, dates, and friends. On the other hand, the non-Jewish white majority were least ethnocentric in choosing friends, showed an increased but equal degree of ethnocentrism in choosing leaders and work partners, and showed their highest degree of ethnocentrism in choosing dates.

One possible explanation of this difference between the majority and the minorities in this respect might be that the majority, feeling secure in its status, can afford the luxury of uninhibited choice of friends, regardless of the minority status of these friends. The minorities, however, do not reciprocate by corresponding freedom on choosing friends from the white majority or from other outgroups. The freedom of choice of friends on the part of the majority group does not extend, however, to the choice of dates, in which relationship they show greater ethnocentrism than Jews and Japanese, but less than the Negroes and the Chinese.

At least part of the explanation of these results may be found in the fact that while the questions regarding leaders, work partners, and dates are hypothetical (*"If* you could have a date with anyone in this school, whom would you choose?"), whereas the question regarding friends asks for a present fact ("Who *are* your best friends?"). For whatever reason (feelings of insecurity, deliberate cultivation of ethnocentrism, and so forth), it remains a significant fact that *our data show, for all minorities, a greater ethnocentrism in the choice of friends than is shown by the majority group.* It may be that the mere fact of being consciously a member of a minority causes one to draw together with other numbers of that minority, and that this tendency becomes more pronounced as the minority is smaller in size. That is, ethnocentrism may be a sort of struggle for cultural survival, becoming more intense as the survival is threatened.[11]

Characteristics associated with outgroup choosing. In spite of the general preference of each ethnic group for leaders, work partners, dates, and friends drawn from their own group, each of the ethnic groups chose *some* of these associates from outgroups. This raises the question: Within each ethnic group, how do persons who make outgroup choices differ from those who make only ingroup choices? For reasons of space only the most general conclusions are presented below.[12]

CHARACTERISTICS OF THE NON-JEWISH WHITES WHO MADE OUT-GROUP CHOICES. Eighteen and eight-tenths percent of the non-Jewish white group chose members of some outgroup for leaders. Twenty-six percent of these outgroup choosers were males, 12.6

[11]This hypothesis is supported by the findings of the study mentioned in footnote 3. A further qualification to the statement italicized above should be made, namely, that the frequent mutual outgroup choosing between *the two white groups* operates to give them relatively low indices of ethnocentrism, which increase if the non-Jewish white and the Jewish groups are combined. For example, the Criswell index for the white group *as a whole* rises to 45 on dating, as against 14.7 and 3.7 (Table 9-I) for non-Jewish whites and Jews, respectively. The ethnocentrism index (Criswell) on the other questions is affected only relatively slightly by the combination of the Jewish with the other white group. A combination of the Japanese and Chinese results in reducing their ethnocentrism index on all questions. Of course this does not contradict the findings as reported above, but does indicate that the pronounced line of cleavage on dating, at least, is the color line.

[12]The full data comprising some 32 tables and 210 computed chi-squares are available in Lenore Dickson, *op. cit.* To answer the question stated above, the outgroup choosers and the ingroup choosers of each ethnic group were compared, by sex, on each of 28 categories representing subclasses of the following characteristics:
1. Age and school class
2. Nationality (Did ancestors come only from northwestern Europe or did they come from some other part of the world?)
3. Membership in organizations (school, church, other organization outside of school)
4. Socioeconomic status (occupation of parents, mother working, student working part-time, living in census tract of known socioeconomic status as determined by 11 indices)
5. Propinquity with Negroes and other minorities
6. Intelligence-intellectualism (membership in scholastic honor society and plans to attend college)

percent females (difference significant at 0.05 level). Similar results (23 percent and 13.9 percent) were found on the question of work partner. On the dating question, the percent of outgroup choices falls to about 10 percent for both sexes with no significant difference in percent of male and female choosers. The lowest ethnocentrism is found among both sexes in choosing friends (males 28.8 percent, females 15 percent), again with a statistically significant difference between the sexes.

Of the 28 factors tested, five were not significantly associated with outgroup choosing by either sex, on any of the four questions. These five factors were church attended, church activities participated in, membership in Masonic organizations, membership in "Y"-sponsored organizations, and whether ancestors came only from northwestern Europe or from some other patr of the world.

None of the factors was significantly associated with outgroup choosing by both sexes on all four questions. The most nearly universally significant factors were membership in a fraternity, sorority, or other exclusive club. Such membership is, among all groups and both sexes, associated with ethnocentrism, with one minor exception, namely, in the case of females choosing leaders. In all other groups and relationships *there was a significant positive association between not belonging to fraternal groups and outgroup choosing.*

A boy was more likely to choose into the outgroup on all four questions if he (a) did not belong to a fraternity or indeed (b) to any club at all outside of school and (c) if he lived in a census tract characterized by a high percent of laborers, persons seeking work, and dwelling units without mechanical refrigeration or central heating.

None of the 28 factors tested was significantly associated with outgroup choosing by the girls on all questions.

The factors chosen for study seemed to function much better in differentiating between boys who chose outgroup members and those who chose only non-Jewish whites than in similarily differentiating between the girls. For the boys a significant association was found in 63 of the 100 chi-square tests made, but for the girls a significant association was found in only 15 of the 104 similar tests. Even excluding the 88 tests pertaining to characteristics of the census tract in which a student lived, the ratio is still 24 significant factors for the boys and only 14 for the girls.

The significance of each of the seven *principal* characteristics here tested for their association with outgroup choosing by the non-Jewish whites may be summarized as follows:

1. *Sex.* On all questions but dating, boys were more likely to make outgroup choices than the girls were. To explain this phenomenon several hypotheses may be advanced. Perhaps boys were less bound by convention than girls, hence, more likely to disregard taboos against interethnic contact. That is, boys may feel more secure and may not be so fearful of losing their own prestige by choosing persons of lower social status. Again, it may be that boys of high school age are less mature than girls, and it has been shown that the younger (i.e. less mature) students are more likely than older ones to choose from the outgroup. Another significant consideration may be the fact that a smaller percent of boys than of girls belong to organizations outside of school, for it has been shown that ethnocentrism is positively correlated with membership in such clubs.

2. *Age and school class.* For each sex and question, a chi-square test was applied first to age and then to class, a total of 16 chi-square tests. In nine of these we found the younger, lower school-class students significantly more likely to make outgroup choices than were their older, junior-senior classmates. This finding that ethnocentrism increases with age has already been pretty well established in other ethnic studies. The explanation usually given is that as part of the process of socialization, children become increasingly aware of the cleavages which exist in the adult world and adjust their own behavior to conform.

3. *Nationality.* For both sexes on all four questions no significant difference was found between the extent of the outgroup choosing by students designating their ancestry as northwestern European as compared with ancestry from some other part of the world.

4. *Membership in organizations.* In 23 out of 53 tests of significance it was found that membership in organizations made for ethnocentrism—that is, that nonmembers were more likely to make

outgroup choices. Excluding the 16 tests pertaining to church organizations, we find 23 out of 37 tests significant. This relationship was especially pronounced in the cases of membership in the more intimate social groups (sororities and fraternities). The data appear to confirm the common-sense generalization that membership in an ingroup, the essence of which is exclusiveness, must limit freedom of choice in outgroups. There was one notable exception to this finding: among girls in choosing leaders, it was the members, not the nonmembers, of the scholastic honor society who were more likely to make outgroup choices. Since membership in the honor society is determined by how well a student does in his studies rather than by his interests or friendships, this finding is not actually an exception to the rule stated above.

5. *Socioeconomic status.* Fifteen different measures of socioeconomic status (11 of them ecological) were tested for each sex on each of the four questions. Of the 60 tests for boys, 45 showed a significant association between low status and outgroup choosing. But of the 60 similar tests for girls, only one was significant. Girls living in census tracts with a high percentage of Negroes were more likely to make outgroup choices than those living elsewhere. This seems to indicate that *all* girls are bound by the social proprieties, but only boys of high status tend to be similarly restricted. There are many possible reasons why high socioeconomic status might be correlated with high ethnocentrism: (a) students living in poorer neighborhoods come into contact with more minority persons; (b) mothers who work outside the home cannot supervise their children's choices of friends as well as housewives can; and (c) students who have jobs themselves do not have time or other resources to join "social" groups, which, as we have seen, operate to restrict frequency of outgroup choices.

6. *Residential propinquity with Negroes and minority students.* In choosing work partners, dates, and friends, boys who lived in census tracts which had a high percentage of Negroes or other minorities were less ethnocentric than those living in other areas. But on leadership, the ethnic composition of a boy's neighborhood was not significantly associated with his ethnocentrism. This may be due to the fact that choosing a leader is not based on personal contact with the person chosen; therefore, the amount of contact

a person has with the outgroup will not influence his leadership choices, but may have a considerable effect on his other choices. The number of Negroes or members of other minorities living in a girl's neighborhood did not significantly influence her ethnocentrism except in one respect: the percent of Negroes in the census tract was positively correlated with the tendency of girls to make outgroup choices of work partners.

7. *Intelligence-intellectualism.* Results were inconclusive on this subject. Of 15 tests made, only three showed a significant degree of association. Girls belonging to the scholastic honor society chose outgroup leaders significantly more than did nonmembers, and boys who did not plan to attend college chose outgroup co-workers and friends significantly more than did the other boys. There seems to have been a definite demarcation between leadership and the other three questions. Intelligent or intellectual students seem to be more likely to evaluate leadership qualities without prejudice. However, this does not seem to carry over into the more intimate situations, which, it may be noted, are usually formed on a less intellectual basis.

To summarize: Among the non-Jewish whites there was a tendency for groups with the following characteristics to make outgroup choices significantly more frequently than was the case in the population as a whole: (a) males, (b) persons under 16 years of age, (c) freshmen and sophomores, (d) persons not belonging to organizations, and (e) boys—but not girls!—with low socioeconomic status.

OUTGROUP CHOICES BY THE MINORITIES. The characteristics of outgroup choosers among the minorities can best be presented in comparison with the findings of the preceding section regarding the characteristics of outgroup choosers among the non-Jewish white majority. (All differences noted are significant at the 0.05 level.)

1. *Sex.* Except for the Japanese, boys were less ethnocentric than girls in all the ethnic groups. This was especially marked in the Negro group where they were significantly less ethnocentric than girls on all four questions.

2. *Class.* With respect to school class, findings for non-Jewish whites were in direct contrast with those for the minorities. In

the non-Jewish white group it was the freshman and sophomore students rather than juniors or seniors who were more likely to make outgroup choices; in the minorities, outgroup choices were most often made by upperclassmen. However, this tendency for minority juniors and seniors to make more outgroup choices than freshman and sophomores was true only on the prestige questions —leadership, work, and dating; class and ethnocentrism of minorities were not significantly associated on friendship. These findings indicate that all students, regardless of whether they belong to the majority or to a minority, give more choices to the majority, on prestige questions, as they advance in school. In other words, as they mature, they acknowledge, and hence reinforce, the prestige of the established leaders.

3. *Age.* In general the same tendencies noticed with respect to class were found true for the different age groups. In the majority group, lower (school) class and younger students were most likely to make outgroup choices; in the minority groups, it was the upper (school) class and older students who made the most outgroup choices. The one exception was that "middle-aged" Jews were more likely than either older or younger ones to choose non-Jews as leaders.

4. *Church attended.* This factor was significantly associated with outgroup choosing only for the ethnic group which was differentiated on the basis of religion—the Jews. Logically enough, it was the Jews who did not attend church who were least ethnocentric in religion.

5. *Office-holding.* Non-Jewish whites who did not hold offices were more likely than officers to make outgroup choices. There was no significant association between outgroup choosing and office holding in the minority groups except that Japanese officers were more likely than nonofficers to choose non-Japanese workpartners, which contradicts the findings for the majority group.

6. *Participation in school activities.* Members of school organizations were more ethnocentric than nonmembers if they were non-Jewish white, Japanese, or Negro, less ethnocentric if they were Chinese, and equally ethnocentric if Jewish.

7. *Plans after graduation.* Non-Jewish white boys who intended to go to college were more ethnocentric than other boys.

Chinese who planned to go to college were less ethnocentric than other Chinese. Plans after graduation and outgroup choosing were not associated for non-Jewish white girls, Japanese, Jews, and Negroes.

On the basis of the above findings, we can roughly classify our factors into two groups: (a) those which make for ethnocentrism in both the majority and minorities, and (b) those which make for ethnocentrism in one, outgroup choosing in the other.

In the first class, we would definitely place sex. Girls were more ethnocentric than boys in all groups except the Japanese. And, tentatively, we would also place here membership in organizations. Being tied up with an ingroup organization—religious in the case of Jews, secular for Japanese, Negroes, and non-Jewish whites— seems to make for less outgroup choosing; the exception to this rule was the tendency for Chinese who belonged to school organizations to be less ethnocentric than nonmembers. This result may be due to the fact that members of the strictly-Chinese Cathy club (which probably wields strong influence) were classified as nonmembers.

In the class of factors which make for opposite tendencies with respect to ethnocentrism in the majority and minority groups, we find class and age. The greater the age and class in school, the greater the ethnocentrism of non-Jewish whites, and the lesser the ethnocentrism of the minorities. Plans after graduation and officeholding may also be placed tentatively in this class. Non-Jewish whites who planned to go to college and Chinese who did not plan on college tended to be more ethnocentric than their opposites; and non-Jewish white officers and Japanese nonofficers also tended to be ethnocentric.

CONCLUSION

The extent to which the facts and conclusions reported above are applicable to other populations in contemporary American society, or, for that matter, to other cultures in other times and places, is of course a matter to be determined by specific studies. To some extent the applicability of the findings of the present study to other populations may be inferred from data in the vol-

uminous literature dealing with different aspects of the subject.[13]
The specific factual findings and conclusions from the present
study have been stated in the previous section. The following
points may be regarded as partly a restatement of these conclusions,
partly a suggestion of hypotheses for further study, and partly
some theoretical observations on the subject as a whole.

1. There probably is no such thing as ethnocentrism or prejudice *in general*. Ethnocentrism or prejudice probably is always
an attitude toward *specific relationship* (e.g. the Negro in the
South may be *preferred* for certain employment).

2. Ethnocentrism or prejudice is not confined to the majority
or the dominant group. These attitudes are frequently stronger
in all the relationships here tested (except leadership) among
minority groups (a) toward the majority (e.g. Negro attitudes
toward whites as friends) and (b) toward other minorities (e.g.
the attitude of Jews toward Japanese and vice versa).

3. While the non-Jewish white majority exhibit ethnocentrism
of various degrees toward the different minorities, there is reason
to believe that this same non-Jewish white group also exhibits
similar or higher degrees of exclusion against particular groups
or classes within their own non-Jewish white group.[14] For example,
a small group of students from an exclusive residential area showed
as great enthocentrism with respect to the rest of the non-Jewish
white group as they showed toward some of the minorities. This
raises the interesting and difficult question as to whether civic
programs aiming to abolish prejudice against certain minorities

[13]Robin M. Williams, Jr., *The Reduction of Intergroup Tensions: A Survey of Research on Problems of Ethnic, Racial, and Religious Group Relations* (Social Science Research Council, 230 Park Avenue, New York, 1947) (Includes bibliography of 223 items.) See also among more recent studies, Leo Silberman and Betty Spice, *Color and Class in Six Liverpool Schools* (University of Liverpool Press, 1950).

[14]Data on the subject will be presented in a subsequent paper reporting on the study mentioned in footnote 3. Since fraternities and sororities are forbidden in these high schools, the data secured on their membership was unreliable. Neverthe-less, Criswell indices for groups admitting membership in sororities and fraternities show definite ethnocentrism. See also Orvis Collins, "Ethnic Behavior in Industry," *American Journal of Sociology, 51*:293-298, 1946, for a striking case of discrimination against a white group. The flagrant discrimination of Irish against "Yankees" re-ported by Collins is precisely of the same type which when it occurs to certain or-ganized minorities becomes the basis for widespread agitation.

should also be directed at equally exclusive or prejudicial behavior within different strata of the majority group. Also, the question may be raised as to the justification of campaigns on behalf of minorities who themselves practice a higher degree of discrimination against the majority group or against other minorities than is practiced against themselves.

It may be, of course, that the discriminations of the minorities against the majority, or against each other, even when it is pronounced, is relatively innocuous to the community, as compared with the converse situation. But any comprehensive study of prejudice, discrimination, and ethnocentrism, per se, must include both aspects. The question of what should be done, if anything, about the group cleavages and prejudices that are found becomes, then, a practical question of what the standards and attitudes of the community demand. Unless, therefore, reform organizations make clear, both to themselves and to others, just what specific discriminations they are out to abolish, and what degree of such discrimination they regard as unwarranted, they may be regarded as largely romantic movements dedicated to the abolition of the universal phenomenon of selective association ("discrimination," "prejudice," unrequited love, and so on as suffered by a particular minority. To the extent, also, that a particular minority is unwilling themselves to abstain from the same types of discrimination as that of which they complain, they merely place themselves in the unfortunate position of seeking special privileges and immunities.

4. Accordingly, it is suggested that future discussion and action on the general subject of race and interethnic relations had better be guided by more intensive inquiry into the precise nature of the relationships that exist with reference to the norms accepted by all parties. Two questions would appear to be relevant: (a) Is the discrimination complained of greater or more unwarranted than that practiced against other particular classes *within the majority group?* If not, should the proposed reform be equally concerned about these other discriminations? (b) Is the discrimination in question of a character recognized by the existing laws, mores, and institutions as clearly within the province of personal preference and choice? The denial to a minority for ethnic or racial reasons

of the right to vote under the present laws and institutions of the United States is clearly one thing. Discriminations of various groups against each other in such relationships as have been studied above is equally certainly another matter.

The traditional freedom of choice of associates in these primary group relationships is quite as fully guaranteed by our laws and constitutions as is the right of citizens to vote. Indeed, there is much evidence that free, spontaneous choice of primary group associates is vital both to personal adjustment and to satisfactory group functioning and productivity. At the same time some fraternal organizations, represented perhaps in their most absurd form by school fraternities and sororities, are probably a nuisance from many community standpoints. As long as such organizations are tolerated, however, and if it can be shown that they practice exactly the same discriminations that become the object of civic attack when practiced by ethnic groups, the ground for singling out the latter for special attention must be clearly indicated. As for the attempts to reform or abolish the discriminations of fraternal organizations, this is about as absurd as to attempt to abolish the wetness of water or the coldness of ice. Since exclusiveness is the essence of fraternal organizations, as indeed it is inherent in the basic concept of "in-group," attempts to abolish the discriminatory behaviors that constitute exclusiveness and at the same time defend the "freedom" of such association is self-contradictory and ridiculous.

The first step in a scientific approach to conflicts between ingroup and outgroups is to recognize that it is hopelessly contradictory for any group (a) to desire to maintain an exclusive group identity *of any kind,* and *at the same time* (b) to expect no differential (discriminatory) behavior toward itself on the basis of precisely the exclusive identity sought. This basic consideration does not abolish either the fact of conflict or the desirability of doing what *may* be done about it, through education, agitation, legislation, and so forth. Recognition of the basic nature of the problem, however, affords the only sound basis for action. Action which seeks to advance *mutually exclusive* values is simply psychopathic.

Thus we are confronted with the unpleasant fact that every gain in the abolition of prejudice may represent a value sacrificed on some other front. The right of a group to exclude from a housing area (from clubs, from employment, from fraternizing and so on) whatever classification of people they wish to exclude, *for whatever reason or lack of reason,* may be neither "rational," "just," "democratic," or conducive to community peace and good feeling. Yet, to deny them this right *may* violate a principle of individual freedom which is still more highly valued by nearly everyone, *including* most of the minority, the race, and the religious or ethnic groups which object to the practice as it operates against themselves. In short, they too value the principle of freedom to discriminate in these matters and merely want exemption from its operation against themselves.[15]

To recognize this fundamental conflict in values is not tantamount either to defending present values or advocating others. The authors of this paper get no satisfaction from any of the discriminations mentioned above or throughout this paper, as well as many others current in our society, and would be glad to see them disappear. We merely point out that the achievement of such a goal involves a *cost* in the incidental abandonment of that set of privileges or freedoms which today constitutes the discriminatory behavior. For it must not be forgotten that these behaviors *constitute values to those who practice the behavior.* As such, the issues of prejudice and discrimination that have been widely heralded as a special problem turns out to be another case of reconciling or choosing between conflicting values.

5. The particular respects in which highly ethnocentric personalities differ from the less ethnocentric requires more intensive study than the comparison on the 28 factors included in the present study. These factors were selected chiefly because of their objectivity and availability, and consequently their suitability for statistical study. In addition, there is needed intensive study of the pathologically ethnocentric personality by whatever methods promise to throw light on the differences that unquestionably exist in different persons regarding their willingness to choose

---

[15]See, for example, the analysis of the conflict of proposed Federal Fair Employment Practices with the Bill of Rights, *Commentary of Donald R. Richberg on S 94* (Pamphlet, To the Senate Committee on Labor and Public Welfare, Oct. 10. 1947).

associates from particular outgroups. Also, the *degree* of ethno-centrism which in a given culture at a given time is regarded as a problem needs to be carefully specified, because a certain amount of ethnocentrism is a normal and necessary ingredient of all group life, i.e. it is the basic characteristic that differentiates one group from another and thus is fundamental to social structure. Ethnocentrism ("discrimination," "prejudice") is, therefore, not in itself necessarily to be regarded as a problem.[16] It is rather a question of determining *what degree* of it (a) is functional for social survival and satisfaction under given conditions or at least (b) is not regarded by a society as a problem in the sense of requiring community action. The amount of discrimination that has been shown to exist in the present study, for example, is not incompatible with the peaceful and efficient functioning of the institution in question.

[16]See Percy Black and Ruth D. Atkins, "Conformity versus Prejudice in White-Negro Populations in the South: Some methodological Considerations," *Journal of Psychology*, 30:109-121, 1950.

III. SOCIOCULTURAL AND PSYCHOLOGICAL CAUSAL FACTORS IN THE DEVELOPMENT OF PREJUDICE

Chapter 10

THE TOLERANT PERSONALITY

JAMES G. MARTIN AND FRANK R. WESTIE

Northern Illinois University   *Indiana University*

Subjects randomly drawn from the population of Indianapolis were classified as "tolerant" or "prejudiced" on the basis of a tolerance-prejudice scale featuring a zero point of group preference. The strongly prejudiced were compared with those substantially neutral or tolerant (clustered around the zero point) with respect to 25 personal and social characteristics. The two categories differed significantly on the following attitude scales: "nationalism," "intolerance of ambiguity," "superstition-pseudoscience," "threat-competition," "F," "religiosity," and "child rearing." Tolerant subjects displayed a significantly higher mean level of educational and occupational status, were less suspicious of politicians, and less venerative of their mothers.

Analysis of the relation of intergroup prejudice and tolerance toward outgroups to syndromes of personality characteristics has been plagued by various methodological difficulties. Prominent among these is the problem of systematically and objectively defining categories of "tolerant" and "prejudiced" subjects. Edward Shils has observed, for example, that in "The Authoritarian Personality," "For the most part 'democrats' are distinguished from 'anti-democrats' through their rejection of a considerable series of illiberal opinions which are the stocks in trade of the Xenophobic fundamentalist. . . ."[2] In other words, classification of a person

---

Note. Reprinted by permission from *American Sociological Review, 24:*521-528, 1959. Financial support by the Indiana University Foundation and Social Science Research Council is gratefully acknowledged. Thanks are due Margaret L. Westie for revising the manuscript.

[1]T. W. Adorno *et al., The Authoritarian Personality* (New York, Harpers, 1950).

[2]Edward A. Shils, "Authoritarianism: 'Right' and Left,'" in Richard Christie and Marie Jahoda (Eds.), *Studies in the Scope and Method of "The Authoritarian Personality"* (Glencoe, Ill., Free Press, 1954), p 29.

as "anti-democratic" is determined by his endorsement of propositions which in effect are the articles of faith of the bigot. Those who do not endorse such items are residually defined as "democratic." This procedure, however, could result in the inclusion of respondents who might be far from tolerant in the sense of having a neutral or disinterested attitude towards some group, particularly in view of the widespread normative approval of various forms of group prejudice.

The concept of group prejudice and the methodology of tolerance-prejudice measurement require a "zero point" of group preference or rejection. An instrument is needed that encompasses the entire range of hypothetical tolerance-prejudice, including a midpoint indicating an absence of either positive or negative prejudice. Such a device would permit valid and consistent classification of subjects for the purpose of personality comparisons, according to scale positions established *prior* to interviewing.

This study attempts to determine the distinguishing personal and social characteristics of persons who are operationally defined as tolerant. Instruments employed in most previous investigations of the problem have been inadequate as yardsticks for the assessment of tolerance, and random sampling of subjects has occurred only with respect to a limited population, namely, college students. The study, therefore, also explores the degree to which many of the findings of previous research on prejudice and personality are valid when different techniques of scaling and sampling are invoked.

THE STUDY DESIGN

Prejudice toward Negroes was measured by means of the Summated Differences Scales.[3] These scales yield scores which, rather than ranging from "prejudice" to "less prejudice," range from extremely negative prejudice to neutrality (as indicated by a zero point) to extremely positive prejudice. Thus assessment of the subjects' attitudes relative to the point of neutrality between "anti-Negro" and "pro-Negro" permitted establishment of two statistical categories of subjects: a "tolerant" category that em-

---

[3]For a full description of this device see: Frank R. Westie, "A Technique for the Measurement of Race Attitudes," *American Sociological Review*, 18:73-78, 1953.

braced those whose scores were only slightly on either side of the zero point, and a "prejudiced" category that encompassed those who were extremely hostile towards Negroes.

The Summated Differences Scales used in this study consisted of "residential" and "position" subscales. The residential scale is designed to establish the degree of residential distance the subject insists upon maintaining btween himself and persons of varying racial and occupational membership. The position scale assesses the degree to which the subject is willing to have persons of various racial and occupational membership occupy positions of power and prestige in the community. The scales require the subject to respond with one of five alternatives to various items of the social distance type. The 192 scale items call for responses to Negroes in a variety of occupations and to whites in these *same* occupations. Whites as well as Negroes were included in the items; the tolerance-prejudice score is a function of the *difference* in response to persons of the same occupation but of different racial designation. Thus prejudice towards whites is measured at the same time as prejudice towards Negroes, or stated otherwise, the scoring provides scale positions for those subjects who are positively prejudiced in favor of Negroes as well as for those who are negatively prejudiced. By the same token, if the subject makes no racial distinction in his response to an item such as "I would be willing to have a *Negro lawyer* live next door to me" and is equally willing (or unwilling, as the case may be) to have a *white lawyer* "live next door to me," the subject would have a Summated Differences score of zero for the pair of items. If the sum of the differences between his responses to each half of all 96 pairs of items used in this research is also zero, then his total tolerance-prejudice score is zero.

The total possible range of scores was —432 to +432. Persons whose scores fell between —70 and +70 were defined as "tolerant."[4] Moreover, the additional requirement was invoked that

---

[4]Of the many terms that have been used to describe persons at the "favorable" end of the continuum of intergroup attitudes, we have chosen the term "tolerant" as the least ambiguous and the easiest to define operationally. The people in our tolerant category are clustered on both sides of the zero point, rather than exactly on it (which would indeed make them "unprejudiced"). Some are slightly more

those in the tolerant category be willing to have at least two of the Negro-in-occupation types "live in his neighborhood." The minimal score requirement for inclusion in the prejudiced category was +175 and was based upon previous application of the scale in Indianapolis. The mean score of the tolerants was +31, while for the prejudiced it was +249.

The universe from which the sample was selected consisted of white adults (21 years of age or older) residing within the city limits of Indianapolis in blocks containing no Negro residents. In the Indianapolis population, as perhaps in most or all American cities, there are relatively few persons who qualify as tolerant in their attitudes towards racial outgroups. This posed a serious sampling problem. It was estimated, on the basis of previous research in Indianapolis, that in order to obtain a minimum N of 50 tolerant persons, it would be necessary to interview a preliminary sample of approximately 500 cases. But lengthy interviewing of such a large number of persons would have been prohibitive. Consequently, the following procedure was employed: All city blocks in Indianapolis, except those in which there were Negro residents, were numbered and a sample of 100 blocks was drawn through the use of tables of random numbers. Every second household on these blocks was visited and the individual respondent was asked to complete a short prejudice scale designed specifically to serve as an initial screening device. This scale, constructed according to the internal consistency method, proved to be quite discriminating in spite of its brevity. Persons who on this scale showed little or no prejudice towards Negroes and persons who displayed very strong prejudice were asked to complete the extended

---

favorable towards whites than toward Negroes, others are slightly more favorable toward Negroes than towards whites, while a few are actually *on* the zero point. All, however, manifest a high degree of tolerance from the standpoint of their willingness to have Negroes live near them and to have them occupy positions of power and prestige in the community.

We realize that knowledge of a person's tolerance with respect to Negroes provides us with imperfect knowledge concerning his generalized tolerance towards outgroups. In the interest of specificity and rigor in separating the two contrasting types, it was necessary to forego the inclusion of other outgroups, although the Summated Differences Scales permit the inclusion of a variety of group-objects in the items.

questionnaire which contained the Summated Differences tolerance-prejudice scale. The subject's score on this lengthy battery
of items determined whether or not he would be included in the
final two categories of "tolerant" and "prejudiced."

From the 429 initial respondents who completed the prognos-
tic scale, 41 persons were found who, on the subsequently administered Summated Differences Scales, qualified for the tolerant
category. Also, 59 subjects with conspicuously high prejudice
scores were selected for purposes of comparison, and they constituted the prejudiced category.[5]

FINDINGS

The tolerant and prejudiced subjects were compared with
respect to 25 personal and social characteristics. These variables
were selected in terms of their sociological and psychological
theoretical relevance regarding the nature of prejudice and tolerance and the relationship between prejudice-tolerance and personality factors. The influence of previous research in this area,
particularly as reported in *The Authoritarian Personality,* is
readily apparent.

A number of scales were constructed by the technique of internal consistency to assess the various personal and social characteristics hypothesized to be related to tolerance. The statistical
data on the significant variables are presented in Table 10-I. Intercorrelations of scale scores are presented in Tables 10-II and 10-
III.

Scores on the nationalism scale. Tolerant subjects were significantly less nationalistic, which suggests that a negative prejudice
towards Negroes is an expression of a more basic ethnocentric

---

[5]A total of 668 households were visited. Of these, 168 were "not at homes" (so
classified after minimum of two unsuccessful call-backs) and 71 refused to complete
the short prejudice scale. Of the 429 persons who completed the short scale, 212
persons appeared sufficiently extreme in their attitudes to justify administration of
the lengthy Summated Differences Scales and the variety of other scales and items
dealing with personal characteristics. Of these 212 cases, 12 refused to fill out the
longer form, and 48 failed to return the questionnaire (where they were left to be
picked up later). Of the 152 who filled out the lengthy form, 13 handed it in incom-
plete. There were 39 subjects who failed to qualify as sufficiently tolerant or prejudiced even after completing the full questionnaire.

TABLE 10-I

COMPARISON OF TOLERANT AND PREJUDICED PERSONS ON SELECTED PERSONAL AND SOCIAL CHARACTERISTICS

Characteristic	Tolerants (N = 41)				Prejudiced (N = 59)				S.E. Diff.	Ob. Diff.	C.R.	Prob.
	Range	X	S.D.	S.E.X.	Range	X	S.D.	S.E.X.				
Nationalism	−16 to + 13	+1.02	6.48	1.03	+16 to − 4	+ 9.06	3.12	.40	1.10	8.04	7.30	<.001
Intolerance of ambiguity	−15 to + 5	−7.41	4.07	.64	+16 to −12	+ 3.79	6.33	.83	1.04	11.20	10.77	<.001
Superstition-pseudoscience	−15 to − 1	−7.85	4.20	.66	+15 to −10	− .19	4.33	.57	.87	7.67	8.81	<.001
Threat-competition orientation	−15 to + 6	−4.68	5.28	.84	+14 to − 7	+ 1.86	5.30	.70	1.10	6.54	5.95	<.001
"F" scale	−15 to + 5	−4.39	4.15	.85	+18 to − 8	+ 5.07	6.25	.82	1.18	9.45	8.01	<.001
Religiosity	−18 to + 18	+5.46	10.11	1.60	+18 to − 1	+11.35	4.98	1.02	1.90	5.89	3.10	<.005
Child rearing attitudes	− 5 to + 4	− .93	2.53	.40	+ 6 to − 5	+ 1.39	2.34	.31	.05	2.32	46.40	<.001
Distrust of politicians item	− 2 to + 2	− .51	1.04	.16	+ 2 to − 2	+ .24	1.08	.14	.22	.75	3.41	<.001
Opinion of mother item	− 2 to + 2	+ .90	.96	.15	+ 2 to − 2	+ 1.29	.84	.17	.22	.39	1.77	<.05
Interest in politics item	− 2 to + 2	− .48	1.17	.19	+ 2 to − 2	+ .16	1.13	.15	.24	.64	2.66	<.01
Occupational status	1 to 5	2.94	1.06	.18	2 to 6	4.33	1.36	.23	.28	1.39	4.96	<.001
Amount of education	7 to 20	14.76	2.92	.46	3 to 19	11.65	3.10	.42	.62	3.11	5.02	<.001

orientation. Evidently the tolerant person is not a "social reductionist": he does not have a strong penchant for rigidly inclusive-exclusive reference groups. Sample scale item: "The worst danger to real Americanism during the last 50 years has come from foreign ideas and agitators."[6] (The level of significance of the difference between the tolerant and prejudiced on this variable is $p<.001$.)

Scores on the intolerance of ambiguity scale. The tolerant category is significantly less "intolerant of ambiguity."[7] Tolerant people appeared able and willing to perceive gradation, variation, and relativity, whereas the prejudiced persons seemed to have a need for absolute dichotomies. Unambiguous solutions are demanded for problems by the prejudiced even where no such solutions appear possible. Rigid, categorical thinking is functionally necessary for stereotyping, prejudgment, and sharp ingroup-outgroup distinctions. On the other hand, the tolerant person seems inclined to recognize that each individual, regardless of group assignment, is unique. Sample scale item: "There are two kinds of women: the pure and the bad." (Level of significance: $p<.001$.)

Scores on the superstition scale. The mean score of the tolerants is significantly lower, which invites the inference that they are inclined to prefer the logical and the rational, while the prejudiced persons subscribed to statements indicating a tendency to accept bizarre, mystical, and superstitious definitions of reality. The relationship here might seem tautological in that in many instances the myths that support prejudice take the form of superstitions. Moreover, terms such as "race" and "blood" have mystical appeal. Sample scale item: "Some fortune tellers can actually predict a person's future by studying the lines of his hands." (Level of significance. $p<.001$.)

Scores on the threat-competition scale. The mean score of the tolerant category is significantly lower on this scale, revealing a capacity for compassion, sympathy, and trust, whereas the response pattern of the prejudiced demonstrates a suspicious, competitive,

---

[6]Complete copies of the scales can be secured from J. G. Martin, Northern Illinois University, DeKalb, Illinois.

[7]Cf. Else Frenkel-Brunswik, "Intolerance of Ambiguity as Emotional and Perceptual Personality Variable," *Journal of Personality*, 18:108-143, 1949.

"jungle" weltanschauung. Tolerant people, the findings indicate, are likely to stress mutual assistance and to give others the benefit of the doubt in making judgments about them. Sample scale item: "If a person doesn't look out for himself, nobody else will." (Level of significance: $p<.001$.)

Scores on the "F" scale. The nine most efficient items from the "F" scale used in *The Authoritarian Personality* study discriminate significantly between the two categories of subjects. Sample scale item: "What the youth needs most is strict discipline, rugged determination, and the will to fight for family and country." (Level of significance: $p<.001$.)

Scores on the religiosity scale. The significantly lower mean score of the tolerant category indicates that the tolerant person tends to reject the fundamentalistic, doctrinaire, and conservative outlook in favor of a more humanistic orientation. This religiosity scale, it should be noted, is essentially a religious conservatism scale, stressing dogma and supernaturalism. Although these results point to the conclusion that there are certain differences in the emotional-intellectual quality of the religious orientation of the two categories of subjects, no significant relationship was found between tolerance and prejudice and frequency of church attendance, praying, Bible reading, and percentage of income contributed to one's religious group. Sample scale item: "Someday Christ will return." (Level of significance: $p<.005$.)

Scores on the child rearing attitudes scale. The tolerant and the extremely prejudiced person were strikingly different in their

TABLE 10-II

CORRELATION MATRIX OF SCALE SCORES OF
TOLERANT SUBJECTS $(N = 41)$

Scale	1	2	3	4	5	6	7
1 Nationalism	X	.22	.39*	.01	.28	.41*	.10
2 Intolerance of ambiguity		X	.37*	—.01	.34*	.32*	.48*
3 Superstition-pseudoscience			X	.24	.40*	.31*	.36*
4 Threat-competition				X	.17	—.08	.28
5 "F"					X	.56*	.62*
6 Religiosity						X	.48*
7 Child rearing							X

*Significantly different from zero at the .05 level.

child rearing attitudes. Tolerants were inclined to reject authoritarian practices stressing strict obedience, harsh discipline, and physical punishment. The strongly prejudiced person endorsed items suggesting a positive view toward force, retribution, conflict, and distrust. He expressed a strong preference for "obedience and respect" in children. Sample scale item: "Obedience is the most important thing a child should learn." (Level of significance: $p < .001$.)

Responses to miscellaneous items and background questions. The differential frequency between tolerant and prejudiced subjects is *not* statistically significant for the following characteristics: parental relations, evaluation of the father, disciplinary atmosphere of the family of orientation, frequency of punishment as child, childhood economic security, attitude towards pessimists, "Menace" choice, and self-image choice. Individuals in the prejudiced category, however, expressed a more venerative attitude towards their mothers ($p < .05$), while the tolerants were less distrustful of politicians ($p < .001$) and more interested in politics ($p < .01$).

The distribution of tolerant and prejudiced subjects by religious affiliation show no significant deviation from chance. The tolerants are slightly overrepresented in the "other," "Catholic," and "none" response cells, as are the prejudiced in the "Protestant" cell. There were no Jewish respondents found in the final sample.

A significantly larger portion of females are in the prejudiced

TABLE 10-III

CORRELATION MATRIX OF SCALE SCORES OF
PREJUDICED SUBJECTS (N = 59)

Scale	1	2	3	4	5	6	7
1 Nationalism	X	.32*	.32*	.22	.28*	.12	.19
2 Intolerance of ambuiguity		X	.54*	.62*	.72*	.13	.29*
3 Superstition-pseudoscience			X	.52*	.58*	.02	.14
4 Threat-competition				X	.70*	—.08	.30*
5 "F"					X	.14	.28*
6 Religiosity						X	.22
7 Child rearing							X

*Significantly different from zero at the .05 level.

category ($p<.005$, according to chi-square analysis). Aside from the implicit reference to Negro males in the tolerance-prejudice scale items—which may or may not be offset by a similar male occupational reference for whites—this finding remains something of an enigma.

Although the two groups did not differ significantly in generational occupational or educational mobility, the distribution of responses suggests that *downward* mobility is associated with prejudice. Tolerant subjects show a significantly higher mean occupational status and educational status ($p<.001$, for both). The modal income was the same for both categories, $4000. This result is noteworthy when one considers that the tolerants enjoyed higher educational and occupational status and expressed less economic insecurity. One surmises that tolerant people are less likely to see themselves as "economically deprived," even where there is a basis for such a view.

DISCUSSION

This research lends confidence to the basic proposition that tolerant persons differ from prejudiced persons in many personal and social respects, and that these discriminating characteristics are sufficiently numerous, pervasive, and fundamental to justify reference to tolerant and prejudiced personality syndromes. Understanding of the finer details of the functional interrelationships among these various characteristics in particular personalities would require clinical study of tolerants, defined and selected at least as carefully as those studied in the present research.

With respect to the characteristics of the prejudiced personality, our findings strongly suggest that many of the insights gained by the authors of *The Authoritarian Personality*, despite the shortcomings of their scaling methods, possess a considerable degree of validity and, despite the sampling shortcomings, probably apply to populations beyond those they studied, at least within comparable regions and subcultures.

However, because studies of personality and prejudice have led to many misunderstandings concerning the nature of both personality "types" and of prejudice, several qualifications should be made explicit. Of course, not every person who "tolerates" outgroups is tolerant of ambiguity, nonnationalistic, gentile in his treatment of children, and so on. The configurations as embodied in actual people are far from perfect matches of the ideal type. This is readily apparent from examination of Tables 10-II and 10-III, which present correlations of each of the scales with each of the others. Although in many instances the intercorrelations are substantial, in other cases the correlations do not qualify as significantly different from zero at the .05 level. But there is a degree of probability, however moderate, that the person who "tolerates" outgroups will also be generally tolerant of ambiguity, nonnationalistic, and so forth. Thus, as in the case of parole prediction devices, the predictive utility of such descriptions is much greater when applied to social groups and categories than when applied to individuals.

Perhaps the most important reason why real-life embodiments of these configurations are so imperfect lies in the fact that prejudice towards outgroups is part of the normative order of American society. Moreover, the degree to which rejection of particular outgroups is approved varies from one subculture to another and from region to region. Not only the community at large but the immediate groups to which the person belongs provide him with definitions of ingroups and outgroups and the "correct" feelings and behaviors in relation to their members. Under such circumstances, we find in our midst many "happy bigots" whose prejudices are born, not so much of personal psychological difficulties, but rather of the fact that their community and various groups inculcate, expect, and approve of their prejudices; personality factors probably serve primarily to predispose and to intensify or abate normative expectations. In such situations, the tolerant person may well be the deviant and a legitimate subject for analysis in terms of abnormal psychology. He may be tolerant because tolerance is deviation, and deviation may be a functionally very important retaliatory mechanism in his personality organization. On the other hand, a person with a considerable "fund of aggression" may be tolerant towards outgroups because his ingroups inculcate and expect tolerance, and although he may be tempted to engage in scapegoating, the negative sanctions may be foreboding. Finally, a person may be tolerant because he has no unusual psychological need to be prejudiced, has been exposed to the broad normative influences in the larger society favorable to tolerance, and does not find the negative sanctions of more local forces a sufficient deterrent to tolerance.[8]

8Although he does not develop extensively the "personality" aspects of these diverse possibilities, their institutional and cultural correlates are suggestively discussed by Robert K. Merton in "Discrimination and the American Creed," in R. M. MacIver (Ed.), *Discrimination and National Welfare* (New York, Harper, 1949), Ch. 11.

Chapter 11

AUTHORITARIAN ATTITUDES IN CHILDREN: I. THE EFFECT OF AGE, IQ, ANXIETY, AND PARENTAL RELIGIOUS ATTITUDES

ARON WOLFE SIEGMAN

University of North Carolina
School of Medicine

PROBLEM AND METHOD

The primary purpose of this investigation was to determine whether authoritarian attitudes in children vary with age. Data were also obtained about the effect of other variables on authoritarian attitudes in children. The present paper reports the findings about the effect of IQ, manifest anxiety, and degree of parental religious observance.

Subjects

The total group of 83 Ss consisted of five age groups: 21 Ss age nine, 15 Ss age ten, 11 Ss age eleven, and 21 Ss age thirteen. The IQ and socioeconomic class distributions of the various age groups were similar, most Ss coming, as determined by Warner's Index of Status Characteristics,[14] from an upper-middle-class background. All Ss were of the Jewish faith.

Note. Reprinted by permission from *The Journal of Clinical Psychology, 13*:338-340, 1957. The data of this study were included in a paper read at the 1956 meeting of the APA in Chicago. The author wishes to express his indebtedness to Mr. Maurice M. Plotnick, Headmaster of the Westchester Day School where this study was conducted, and also to the teaching staff and students for making this study possible. The author is now at Bar-Ilan University, Tel Aviv, Israel.

Procedure

All Ss completed the Children's Authoritarianism Scale (CAS) and the Children's Manifest Anxiety Schedule (MAS) without indicating their names, in order to minimize defensiveness. The answer sheets, however, were coded and their authorship was known to E. The CAS consists of items collected and constructed by Gough et al.[6] The items of the Children's MAS,[12] a rationally constructed questionnaire with apparent content validity, cover the typical childhood fears of animals, the dark and so forth, as well as the usual overt manifestations of anxiety such as restlessness, excessive sweating, and so on. All Ss in age groups ten years and higher were administered the verbal subtests of the WISC. Finally, on the basis of an extensive interview the parents of all Ss were rated on a religious-observance rating scale which ranged from completely nonobservant to strictly observant.

RESULTS AND DISCUSSION

Although scores on CAS did not vary with sex, they did vary significantly with age ($F = 3.01$, $4/78$ df), decreasing with each successive age level. Two hypotheses may be offered in explanation of this finding. One, that the decrease in authoritarian attitudes is due to a maturation of S's cognitive processes. Frenkel-Brunswik[5] has suggested that intolerance of ambiguity, which in the cognitive sphere is expressed by "black and whites" stereotyping, is a key variable in the authoritarian personality. Other work,[2,8,12] however, suggests that "black and white" stereotyping decreases with age, which may account for the decrease in authoritarian attitudes with age. A weak link in this hypothesis, however, is the assumption of a significant relationship between intolerance of ambiguity and authoritarianism, which, although supported by some findings,[9] has been challenged.[4,11]

A number of investigations[1,7,10,12] suggest that the nature of the parent-child relationship is a significant variable in the development of authoritarian attitudes in children, as where a positive correlation between dependency on parental authority and authoritarian attitudes was obtained.[12] Thus, an alternative hypothesis for the decrease in authoritarian attitudes with age may be that it

TABLE 11-I
VERBAL IQ SCORES IN RELATION TO CAS SCORES

Group	N	Mean	SD	t	p
High CAS scorers	16	111.25	10.20		
Low CAS scorers	16	122.00	10.73	3.27	<.01

is a function of an increasing independence of parental authority
with age. It may well be that both hypotheses are valid, and perhaps in different segments of the age continuum represented in
the present sample.

Ss who scored in the upper quartile of the CAS distribution
and Ss who scored in the lower quartile of this distribution were
compared in relation to their verbal IQ scores. The two groups
were equated for age. Table 11-I indicates that Ss who were high
on the CAS obtained significantly lower verbal IQ scores. This
finding is consistent with what has been reported by others[3,10] and
points to a cognitive factor in authoritarian attitudes. Moreover,
it supports the hypothesis that the decrease in authoritarian attitudes with age may be partly a function of a maturational development of cognitive processes.

Ss who scored in the upper third of the MAS distribution and
Ss who scored in the lower third of this distribution were compared in relation to their scores on the CAS. Again the two groups
were equated for age. Table 11-II indicates that the high MAS
scores also obtained significantly higher CAS scores. This finding is consistent with what has been found in adult populations[3]
and suggests that, in addition to cognitive factors, personality
factors are also a significant source of variance in authoritarian
attitudes.

Finally, significantly more Ss from religiously strictly observant
homes obtained scores in the upper and lower quartiles of the CAS

TABLE 11-II
CAS SCORES IN RELATION TO MAS SCORES

Group	N	Mean	SD	t	p
High MAS scorers	26	9.81	2.97		
Low MAS scorers	26	4.58	2.73	6.62	<.001

TABLE 11-III

DISTRIBUTION OF CAS SCORES IN RELATION TO
RELIGIOUS OBSERVANCE

| Group | CAS Scores Distribution | | Chi-Square | p |
	Upper and Lower Quartile	Middle Quartile		
Very observant	13	5		
Nonobservant	9	9	3.56	<.05

distribution than did Ss from nonobservant homes (Table 11-III). The age distribution of the two groups was about the same. More important than indicating the significance of parental attitudes in the development of authoritarian attitudes in children is the empirical, though indirect, evidence that the relationship between religious observance and authoritarianism is a curvilinear one. Similar finding has been reported[1,13] in relation to ethnic prejudice. This curvilinear relationship between religious influence and authoritarian and ethnic attitudes may be a function of a paradox which is characteristic of many religions. On the one hand they are committed to "social justice" and consequently to social change, but on the other hand they also tend to foster an atmosphere inimical to social change. This duality may in turn differentially reinforce diametrically opposed attitudes and personality dispositions.

SUMMARY

The Children's Antidemocratic Scale (CAS) was administered to 83 Ss with an age range of nine to thirteen. Ss' CAS scores decreased significantly with age. It was suggested that the decrease in authoritarian attitudes with age is due to the maturation of Ss' cognitive processes as well as Ss' increasing independence of parental authority. Ss with high CAS scores obtained significantly lower verbal IQ scores and significantly higher scores on the Children's Manifest Anxiety Schedule than those with low CAS scores. Finally, Ss whose parents were strictly observant of the Jewish religion tended to fall either in the upper or the lower quartile of the CAS distribution.

REFERENCES

1. ALLPORT, G. W., and KRAMER, B. M.: Some roots of prejudice. *J. Psychol.*, *22*:9-39, 1946.
2. AMES, L. B., LEARNED, J., METRAUX, R., and WALKER, R. N.: *Child Rorschach Responses: Developmental Trends from Two to Ten Years.* New York, Hoeber, 1952.
3. DAVIDS, A.: Some personality and intellectual correlates of intoleranc of ambiguity. *J. Abnorm. Soc. Psychol.*, *51*:415-420, 1955.
4. DAVIDS, A.: The influence of ego-involvement on relations between authoritarianism and intolerance of ambiguity. *J. Consult. Psychol.*, *20*:179-184, 1956.
5. FRENKEL-BRUNSWIK, E.: Intolerance of ambiguity as a personality variable. *Amer. Psychol*, *3*:268, 1948, (Abstract)
6. GOUGH, H. G., HARRIS, D. B., MARTIN, W. E., and EDWARDS, M.: Children's ethnic attitudes: I. Relationship to certain personality factors. *Child. Devel.*, *21*:83-91, 1950.
7. HARRIS, D. B., GOUGH, H. G., and MARTIN, W. E.: Children's ethnic attitudes: II. Relationship to parental beliefs concerning child training. *Child. Devel.*, *21*:169-183, 1950.
8. L'ABATE, L.: Sanford's uncertainty hypothesis in children. *Amer. Psychol.*, *11*:415, 1956, (Abstract)
9. LEVITT, E. E.: Studies in intolerance of ambiguity: I. The Decision-Location Test with grade school children. *Child. Develop.*, *24*: 263-268, 1953.
10. LYLE JR., W. H., and LEVITT, E. E.: Punitiveness, authoritarianism, and parental discipline of grade school children. *J. Abnorm. Soc. Psychol.*, *51*:42-46, 1955.
11. McCANDLESS, B. R., and HOLLOWAY, H. D.: Race prejudice and intolerance of ambiguity in children. *J. Abnorm. Soc. Psychol.*, *51*:692-693, 1955.
12. SIEGMAN, A. W.: Some Factors Associated with Authoritarian Attitudes in Children. Paper read at Amer. Psychol. Ass., Chicago, September, 1956.
13. SIEGMAN, A. W.: Variables Associated with Anti-Negro Bias in Children. Paper read at Eastern Psychol. Ass., New York City, March, 1957.
14. WARNER, W. L., MEEKER, MARCIA, and EELLS, K.: *Social Class in America.* Chicago, Science Research Associates, Inc., 1949.

Chapter 12

CHILDREN'S CONCEPTS AND ATTITUDES ABOUT MINORITY AND MAJORITY AMERICAN GROUPS

Marian Radke

Formerly Research Center for Group Dynamics,
Massachusetts Institute of Technology

AND

Jean Sutherland

Wheelock College
Boston, Massachusetts

Early in their lives children learn to use the word "American" and, in time, to identify themselves as "American." It is a crucial identification, for it is eventually bound up with the individual's behavior and attitudes in many areas of social living. He views the world as an American; he has certain rights and duties and loyalties as an American; and his attitudes toward himself and others are partly a matter of being an American. But "American" is a concept applied liberally and easily, and even a casual study of children's conversation reveals that it includes many confused and erroneous ideas.

The problem of this research is to study the meaning of "American" to children of school age, and to discover, if possible, some of the sources from which their concepts of American develop. The specific questions raised in the study are as follows: (a) In what dimensions is American perceived? (b) What values or attitudes are linked with American? (c) What group differentiations are made, i.e. from what groups is American differentiated? Which subgroups are included in American and which preclude

---
Note. Reprinted by permission from *The Journal of Educational Psychology,* *40*:449-468, 1949.

being American? Can children conceive of subgroups which are different from themselves but which belong to the same inclusive American group?

To obtain data on these problems, children were questioned concerning their own inclusive American group and two American minority groups to which the children do not belong, Jewish and Negro. A written questionnaire was used which asked for the meaning of each group and for explanations or rationalizations for the meanings given.

SUBJECTS

Two hundred and seventy-five children of grades V through XII were studied. This number constituted the entire public school population of these grades in a small midwestern town. The town of several thousand inhabitants is like many midwestern communities—strikingly homogeneous in cultural background and social mores. There is an air of prosperity about it. The several industries and small businesses furnish moderate, comfortable incomes for the residents. Though outside easy commuting distance, it lies within the orbit of several large urban centers. The majority of the population is German-American of the second, third, and fourth generations, with a small percentage of the population of English, Scandinavian, and southern European descent. The community is predominantly Protestant. There is a recognizable Catholic minority. There is only one childless Jewish family. There are no Negroes in the town.

The children studied are similar in social and cultural backgrounds. They have had a minimum of personal experience with the two minority groups, fairly similar kinds of religious training, and the same school experience.

QUESTIONNAIRE

The questionnaire was administered in school to each class by the teacher. The instructions given by the teacher were as follows:

Our school has been asked to help in a study of what school children (high school students) think about various groups of

American people. To do this, we are asked to answer some questions.

You will not be graded on these papers You will not put your name on these papers. Your answers will not be read by the teachers. Your answers will be added to the answers of other children (students).

These are the questions about several groups of American people:

1. What do you think Americans are like? What makes you think so?

2. What do you think Negroes are like? What makes you think so?

3. What do you think Jews are like? What makes you think so?

Write what you know and think about each question. Don't make up answers if you don't know. Give your own ideas. You will have twenty-five minutes to answer the questions."

The questions were phrased "What are Americans like?" rather than "What are Americans?" because it was found in preliminary questioning that the first form brought out, in addition to cognitive structure, many more value statements and comparisons of one group with another. This form of question has several advantages over a checklist of words from which the subject selects those words which he considers most appropriate for describing a group. The child must draw completely on his own ideas and formulate the description himself. In his formulation, his level of understanding and his feelings are often clearly revealed.

In asking "What makes you think so?" it was not expected that the children could supply the actual sources of their information and attitudes (except occasionally), but that in attempting to support their statements an indication would be given of the kind of justifications and experiences which accompany various kinds of concepts and attitudes.

Responses were analyzed by breaking down each answer into its component ideas. The frequency of the separate items and of the various patterns of items appearing in the responses are reported. In each case the percentages represent the percentage of children who answered in the given category.

Responses to the Question "What Are Americans Like?"

Responses to the question "What are Americans like?" fall into four general categories:

1. *Democratic ideology and patriotism.* "They are democratic and have the best form of government." "They have freedom of worship and speech." "I think they should be all treated alike."

2. *Kinds of people, in racial or cultural terms.* "They are many people of different nationalities." "Americans belong to the white race." "People are classified in different groups—some wealthy and stuck-up, they look down on poor people. Some wealthy help poorer people along."

3. *A comparison of Americans with other peoples.* "I think Americans are just as good as any other people in other countries." "Americans are or rather think they are superior than most other people." "They are becoming the leader of the world."

4. *Personal characteristics.* "They are honest and well educated—they are clean." "They are stingy and only think of themselves." "They are kind to one another and to their neighbors."

The reliability of this method of categorizing responses to all the questions was measured by the percentage of agreement of two independent codings of 85 questions. The results are as follows:

"What are Americans (Negroes, Jews) like?" 92.8 percent

"What makes you think so?" 89.4 percent

Table 12-I presents the responses to the question on the meaning of American. There is a striking lack of ideological content here. While there are many stereotypes which concern the individual behavior of Americans ("They're rugged," "They're go-getters," "They are ambitious"), there are few group goals or values in evidence. The comments on American ideals or democratic government are mainly clichés such as "Americans are in a land for the free and the brave" or "Americans are loyal." Freedom as an aspect of American life has a variety of meanings which are often imbedded in the daily experiences of the children ("Americans are free to choose the friends they want") as well in the more remote areas of their lives ("They have freedom of

TABLE 12-I

WHAT ARE AMERICANS LIKE?
(Percentage of Children)

Descriptions	Grades			
	5–6 (N = 50)	7–8 (N = 68)	9–10 (N = 95)	11–12 (N = 62)
Democratic ideology, patriotism				
Have many freedoms	12	22	24	10
Government by people	4	3	1	3
People loyal to government	14	36	13	11
Kinds of people				
Mixed nationalities	2	7	8	8
White people	6	2	1	0
Rich and poor	4	3	1	3
Comparison with other peoples				
Like others	28	25	7	13
Different from others	0	2	1	2
Better than others	4	12	12	16
A powerful nation	2	3	3	8
Personal characteristics				
Ambitious, energetic, achieving	20	19	31	46
Kind, honest, friendly	64	65	41	31
Clean	4	4	5	0
Educated, intelligent	4	12	14	19
Carefree	0	2	4	16
Religious	0	6	1	0
Value money, material possessions	4	6	11	13
Criticism of personal characteristics	6	16	15	21

press"). The variety of meanings attached to freedom are listed below:

	Frequency
To value and appreciate freedoms	12
To do as they please	10
To fight to keep free	9
To hate dictators, don't like to be ordered around	4
To have many freedoms other countries don't have	3
To have freedom of speech and press	3
The right to own religious beliefs	3
The right to choose friends	1
The right to eat what you want	1
Negroes want to be free	1

When Americans are compared with other peoples, the other groups are usually unspecified, and Americans are perceived as different from, on a par with, or better than others. A decreasing proportion of children make statements of equality 28 percent,

25 percent, 7 percent, 13 percent) from the fifth and sixth to the eleventh and twelfth grades. Increasing with age are feelings about the superiority of Americans over other people (4 percent, 12 percent, 12 percent, 16 percent). Examples of this chauvinism at the younger and older age levels are quoted below:

I think Americans are smart. They know more than the Negroes. (sixth grade)

Americans are the best people of the races, they are Democrats and have the best form of government. They are easygoing, make friends easily, and are the most prized people in foreign nations. (twelfth grade)

The greatest number of responses are about personal characteristics. There are two clusters of traits: One is the bland and admirable qualities of nice, kind, friendly, honest, generous—which are found especially at the younger age levels (64 percent at grades V and VI, and 31 percent at grades XI and XII). The second group of traits which increases in frequency with age (from 20 percent to 46 percent) has in common certain aggressive qualities—energetic, ambitious. Descriptions of Americans as educated people and as having material values appear more frequently in the older children than in the younger. Few personal descriptions are derogatory or critical; however, criticisms increase with age. They are of the following variety:

Americans are	Frequency
conceited and selfish	11
lawless and criminal	13
wasteful and extravagant	5
unfriendly and uncoöperative	6
prejudiced against different races	3
bad morally	2
take democracy for granted	2

Compared with the frequency and intensity of derogatory and rejective responses toward Negro and Jewish American minorities, the infrequency and scatter of criticisms on American stand in sharp contrast.

The descriptions of American do not reveal a highly structured group concept; stereotypes are varied but with the predominance of the "ambitious individualist"; the affect toward American is generally positive with little real criticism involved; and rarely is American differentiated from other groups of people. However, when the limits of the children's concepts of American are tested by asking for descriptions of minority groups, the boundaries of American are more clearly defined, and it becomes apparent that the ideals of freedom and the personal qualities of ambition and the like, are meant to apply to a restricted population.

Responses to the Questions "What Are Negroes Like?" "What Are Jews Like?

Descriptions of Negroes and Jews have been categorized as follows:

1. *Group seen in terms of social problem.* "They should be put in their place or where they came from. We do not want them nor did we bring them." "They have been chased around so much. They haven't had a chance." "They are picked on by the whites."

2. *Group described by a comparison of peoples.* "I think Jews are just another part of the American race." "I think Negroes are just like any other people except for their color." "They are not as progressive as Americans."

3. *An affective reaction expressed toward the group.* "I don't like Jews at all." "I think a good Negro is a dead Negro." "Jews are OK."

4. *Historical or cultural facts given.* "They came from Africa originally and are now in the U.S." "They have a different religion."

5. *Personal or group characteristics ascribed to group.* "Cheaters." "Negroes are dirty, not colert." "Selfish, hard to get along with."

The instructions preceding the questionnaire presented all groups as Americans, although the form of the questionnaire tends to weaken this structuring. With these conditions of questioning, category 2 is significant. (See Table 12-II.) Slightly more than half the children describe Negroes in comparative terms, and about one third, Jews in these terms. About 10 percent of the children describe Negroes as Americans, and between 5 percent and 10 percent describe Jews as Americans, too.

> He is a colored man or woman that came from Africa and is now an American. (eleventh grade)
> I think Jews are just another part of the American race. I think they are all right even though I don't agree with their religion, but that is their own business. (tenth grade)

Another 25 percent to 30 percent perceive Negroes as "like anyone else" except for color of skin; and about 15 percent perceive Jews as like anyone else.

> I think Negroes are just like any other people except the color of their skins and the way they work. I also think they would make better citizens if they were treated right. (tenth grade)
> Jews are just like any other race or class . . . (tenth grade)

There is a small steady rise with age in the proportion of children who say that Negroes are not Americans (4 percent in the

TABLE 12-II

"WHAT ARE NEGROES LIKE?" "WHAT ARE JEWS LIKE?"
(Percentage of Children)

Grades	Negroes				Jews			
Descriptions in terms of	5–6	7–8	9–10	11–12	5–6	7–8	9–10	11–12
Social problem								
Support discrimination	0	3	14	19	2	7	15	11
"Oppose" discrimination, but keep group "in its place"	0	0	1	3	0	0	1	0
Aware of discrimination (attitude not expressed)	0	7	7	14	4	6	7	13
Oppose discrimination	12	39	19	23	4	13	4	11
Comparison with other people								
Americans, too	10	15	6	6	10	7	2	6
Like everyone else except skin color or religion	28	36	20	23	18	16	12	13
Different from Americans but as good	16	10	5	6	4	4	2	2
Different from Americans	4	4	11	11	6	0	2	0
Different from Americans and not as good	0	2	3	11	2	0	3	2
Affect toward group								
"I like them; they're all right"	2	4	13	8	2	2	5	6
"I don't like them"	0	3	5	10	6	4	7	13
"I hate them; eliminate them'	0	0	1	5	0	6	3	6
Historical events or facts	6	9	1	2	2	7	3	5
Personal or group characteristics	76	83	87	91	84	80	80	85

fifth and sixth grades to 11 percent in the eleventh and twelfth grades) or are not as good as Americans (zero percent in the fifth and sixth grades to 11 percent in the eleventh and twelfth grades). The corresponding categories appear infrequently in descriptions of Jews (about 2 percent in each category).

It is significant that many of the children in describing Jews and Negroes are unable to do so for either group without first putting on record their own feeling toward them. The feeling is then "justified" by the addition of various undesirable characteristics as if to prove the right for disliking or discriminating.

> I don't like Jews. In one way they are smart—this is in making money. Many Jews are now running America. I don't think they should be allowed to do this, later they will want to run the whole world. (tenth grade)
>
> Jews are a kind of people I do not like. You find them owning all the large business or selling rags. Never doing real manual labor. (twelfth grade)

If the effect is positive, the supporting reason is more often in terms of standards of respect for all persons or democratic ideology. Thus:

> Jews are just like anyone else. All men are created equal. (seventh grade)

Statements of dislike increase with age for both minority groups. Statements showing accepting attitudes, however, show no consistent age trend. The frequency of negative attitudes within any one age compared with the frequency of positive attitudes reveals that negative expressions occur more often than positive expressions toward the Negro group at the highest grades, and toward the Jewish group at all ages.

Some of the most violent reactions of dislike are quoted below. They appear exclusively above the sixth grade. More statements of this kind are made concerning Jews than Negroes.

> Negroes are a people who think nothing of whites' rights. Negroes are the worst type of people there are, especially when it comes to sex offenses, crime, etc. Get rid of them. (twelfth grade)
>
> The Jew, well there's no room for them and me in this

country; either they're kicked out or I'm willing to go shoot 'em all. (twelfth grade)

I think a dead Negro is a good Negro. (twelfth grade)

Jews are the worst people on earth. Money-hoggers. Worst people in America. I'd like to wring their necks. (ninth grade)

They're [Jews] cheaters, they can cheat you out of one-cent things. There are lots of other things I think about them that I could not write on this piece of paper. (seventh grade)

I think everyone of them [Jews] ought to be shot or else tarred and feathered and ridden out of this country on a rail. (twelfth grade)

The responses of acceptance or rejection of either group are sometimes made with consciousness of the social import of various kinds of group relations. Awareness of a social problem requires more maturity than a simple statement of "I like" or "I don't like," and one would expect responses of this order more frequently in the older than the younger age levels. This is borne out in Table 12-II in the responses under the category of "a social problem."

Recognition of a social problem does not preclude prejudiced attitudes. There is explicit support of discrimination against minority Americans, which increases with age. None of the children in the lowest grades support discrimination against Negroes; 2 percent support discrimination against Jews. At the highest grades the corresponding percentages are 22 percent for Negroes and 11 percent for Jews. A child's response which falls in this category follows:

The Jews are different from Negroes. The Jews are breaking down our government and therefore they should be put in their place or where they came from. If possible give them Germany. . . . They are not American and this country is for Americans. (ninth grade)

When the other side of the coin is examined—how many children explicitly oppose discrimination—the age trends are unsteady, though also increasing with age. The percentage of children opposing discrimination rises from 12 percent in grades V and VI to 23 percent in grades XI and XII in responses concerning Negroes, and from 4 percent to 11 percent in the same grades in responses concerning Jews. Examples of this point of view follow:

The Negroes to me are people just like I am only subjected to a crueller society by the white race. I want the Negroes to have the same advantages that I enjoy in social and economic life. I do not want to see him rise above me in government for some day at their birth rate they would control a country which belongs to the whites. (eleventh grade)

Negroes are like any other person and should be treated that way. (seventh grade)

Most of the children ascribe personal or group traits to the minority groups. There are favorable characteristics ("fine," "good," "intelligent" people), such as the traits ascribed to American, but there are many more which are derogatory in nature. The distribution of traits ascribed to Negroes and Jews by children of each grade is given in Table 12-III.

Inferior traits are most frequently ascribed to the Negro. This tendency increases with age. Similarly "bad" traits assigned to the Negro increase in frequency with age. Jews are most often described in terms of "bad" characteristics, and again there is an increase with age. Descriptions of Jews seldom imply inferiority.

The traits in each of the categories are itemized in Table 12-IV. Between one third and one fourth of the subjects give some favorable quality in their descriptions, such as Negroes "are fine" or "good citizens." With minor exceptions, the remaining traits are uncomplimentary. Patronizing statements are made (Negroes are "gentle," "obedient," "polite") by 17 percent and 11 percent of the younger and older children, respectively. Negro "inferiority" to whites appears especially in the responses of the older children (29 percent). The stereotypes of behavior ascribed to Negroes resemble closely the common stereotypes of the Negro in

TABLE 12-III

TRAITS ASCRIBED TO THE MINORITY GROUPS
(Percentage of Children)

Traits	Ascribed to Negroes (Percent)				Ascribed to Jews (Percent)			
	5–6	7–8	9–10	11–12	5–6	7–8	9–10	11–12
Favorable	34	36	27	21	20	13	13	16
Inferior	26	41	39	67	4	4	3	8
Bad	0	18	23	27	50	45	69	80
Peculiar, unique	22	10	12	25	22	21	7	5

TABLE 12-IV

CHARACTERISTICS ASCRIBED TO THE MINORITY GROUPS
(Percentage of Children)

Characteristics Ascribed	To Negroes Grades		To Jews Grades	
	5–8	9–12	5–8	9–12
Fine, respected, intelligent	36	24	16	14
(Patronizing)—polite, gentle	17	11	0	0
Inferior to whites (non-Jews)	10	29	4	5
Look different	13	4	0	1
Need to be controlled	0	8	3	8
Revengeful, prejudiced against whites	2	6	0	0
Slow, lazy, unambitious	4	20	2	5
Hostile, tough, unfriendly	5	10	0	0
To be feared	2	14	10	15
Stupid, superstitious	4	9	0	0
Bad morals, criminals	3	3	0	0
Sneaky, sly, dishonest	0	3	12	9
Money-making, money-grabbing	0	0	23	44
Greedy, miserly, stingy	0	0	8	11
Aggressive	0	0	5	4
Dirty	3	8	3	1
Like slaves, savages	0	3	0	0
Can endure hard work	2	6	0	0
Sell junk	0	0	10	1
Different speech, manners	1	1	3	1
Lack education, opportunities	10	10	0	0
Disloyal to America	0	0	4	2
Musical	0	3	0	0
Religious	0	5	3	1
Not religious	1	0	2	3

the adult white population.[1] Descriptions of the group as slow, lazy, unambitious, and as tough, insolent, hostile predominate. While the frequencies of the other traits are low, the list includes the familiar prejudiced descriptions: dirty, unintelligent, bad morals.

There is somewhat less variation in the traits assigned to Jews. A large proportion (31 percent and 55 percent of the younger and older children, respectively) appear in the area of dishonest, greedy practices with regard to money. The remaining characteristics are again similar to the stereotypes of the adult anti-Semite —stereotypes of aggressiveness, disloyalty, domination of the country. Religion is mentioned infrequently. Favorable descriptions are given much less frequently than for the Negro, by 10 percent

---

[1]D. Katz and K. Braly, "Racial Stereotypes of 110 College Students," *Abnorm. Soc. Psycho.* 28:280-90, 1933.

and 15 percent of the younger and older children, respectively.
A peculiar sterotype which occurs is that Jews "sells rags and
junk" (14 percent, 7 percent, zero percent, 3 percent for the grade,
respectively). This idea probably goes along with the stereotype
of "money:" a picture of bargaining, cheating, dealing in money
and goods.

It appears that before a group of people has reality to the child,
the group label has long been used as an adjective, an emotionally
toned word, or synonymous with a specific action or state of af-
fairs: you "jew them down"; "there's junk for the Jew"; you get
"dirty like a nigger." These are the experiences in the young
child's life out of which a group attitude grows. "Jewish group"
is an abstraction. When it is first met as an abstraction or in the
form of a person so labeled there are already feelings for the label,
and similarly for the Negro group. With this kind of beginning
for the concepts, it is easy to see how the groups are perceived as
"not American" by virtue of their "badness."

A small proportion of the subjects express fear of either group.
This fear is of one sort when it appears with regard to the Jewish
group, namely, fear that Jews are dominating the government and
business. When fear is expressed about Negroes it concerns the
possibility of their trying to get "revenge" on the whites, or it is
again a fear of governmental domination, but not identical with
this fear expressed in regard to Jews. The difference appears in
the following quotations:

> Jews think they can run the country.
> They'd like to rule the earth.
> They control business in the United States.
> They're too powerful.
> Negroes are trying to rise above us in government.
> They'd like to run people.
> They can't be trusted.
> They can't be trusted to act and talk civilized.
> They'll try for revenge.
> They think nothing of whites' rights.
> The South has a hard time controlling them and their bad
habits.

The great number of derogatory descriptions occurring with
reference to Negroes and Jews contrast markedly with the number

of criticisms of Americans. The three groups are compared below in the ratio of negative statements to neutral or positive statements expressed about each group. These ratios show not only the preponderance of positive statements for American and the slim margin of positive statements for both minorities, but also the tendency for the positive margin to decrease with age.

Ratios of negative to positive statements for:

Grades	American	Negro	Jew
5– 6	1:31	1:39	1:1
7– 8	1:15	1: 5	1:1
9–10	1: 8	1: 3	1: .6
11–12	1:10	1: 2	1: .6

Patterns of Responses Regarding Negroes and Jews

The majority of children gave more than one idea in response to each group. The several ideas expressed by the child about a given group present sometimes a consistent attitude and sometimes a mixture or contradiction of feelings and opinions. Each child's answer was rated on the total of his ideas about each minority: whether he expresses wholly positive, neutral, or negative attitudes or a mixture of positive and negative feelings (Table 12-V). The patterns reveal the following data: Children give completely positive descriptions more frequently at the younger than at the older ages, and more frequently for Negroes than for Jews. Many of the responses in the positive pattern are rather nondescript—"They are kind" and "They are clean." They are not as positive in accepting the group as the negative categories are condemnatory.

TABLE 12-V

PATTERNS OF RESPONSES TOWARD MINORITY GROUPS
(Percentage of Children)

		Toward Negroes				Toward Jews			
	Grades	5–6	7–8	9–10	11–12	5–6	7–8	9–10	11–12
Positive		66	50	40	36	40	43	18	27
Neutral		6	3	6	5	12	4	9	5
Inferior		26	16	20	18	0	0	2	0
Bad and inferior		0	4	14	21	0	0	0	0
Bad		0	0	0	0	32	25	34	39
Conflict: good, bad, inferior		0	22	13	18	12	12	26	19
Don't know and omits		2	4	7	3	4	16	11	10

Patterns of responses which describe Negroes as inferior occur often. Both patterns of "inferior" and "bad" for the Negro increase through the grades. The pattern of "bad" traits ascribed to Jews holds a fairly steady one-third proportion at all grades.

Although answers reflecting conflict might be expected to show an increase through the grades, there is no consistent trend. Conflict responses in most cases are better designated as contradictions, for the child does not seem aware of or disturbed by the contradictory points of view he expresses, thus:

> Because some are very poor. Can't find work because they are a Jew. Some practically run some whole cities. I think if the government doesn't watch them pretty soon they'll be running the whole country. (ninth grade)

The truly "conflict" responses, such as the following, occur infrequently (This response has in it evidences of guilt over the incompatible views expressed.):

> America was founded for the reason of peace. Until some thought that they could take it out on this peace-loving nation by bringing in different races and people who are not wanted in other countries, although America was founded for this reason. (tenth grade)

Patterns of responses on the questionnaires were evaluated also with attention to the correspondence among attitudes expressed toward the three groups by each child. If a child expresses prejudice against one minority group, is he likely to show a similar attitude toward the other? The following percentages of children give negative responses to one or both minority groups:

> 46 percent at grades 5–6
> 53 percent at grades 7–8
> 68 percent at grades 9–10
> 68 percent at grades 11–12.

Of these children, the following percentages reject both minority groups:

> 17 percent at grades 5–6
> 33 percent at grades 7–8
> 48 percent at grades 9–10
> 60 percent at grades 11–12.

Thus, there is an increase in age not only in the percentage of children who describe one or the other minority group in negative terms, but also in the percentage of children expressing dislike who do so for both groups.

Responses on "American" and accompanying reactions to minorities were studied. Responses to American were classed in four categories: boastful chauvinistic attitudes, descriptions of pride and good feeling, description of superficial and trivial aspects of American, and mainly critical responses. No relationships were found between these variations and descriptions of Negro and Jewish groups. The children for whom Americans are "the best that ever was" hold attitudes toward the minorities which are sometimes wholly condemnatory and sometimes completely accepting. Conversely, and it should be of especial importance in education, the child can express the philosophy of democracy and freedom in their concept of American and yet not apply these principles to American minority groups.

> Americans are a people that want to be free and independent and have a democracy for a form of government . . . so the common people have something to say.
> Negroes are black people. They seem funny when you see them. I always get the idea that I don't like them very well.
> I always thought they were a people that sometimes cheat people. (tenth grade)

The generalization of democracy, well spoken, is no guarantee of its application to persons or groups who deviate from the child's own ingroup.

Sources for Responses on Groups

The subjects found it difficult to explain or justify the bases of their concepts or attitudes. When asked "What makes you think so?" their replies are often vague and nonspecific (Table 12-VI). Most frequently they reply with further elaborations of the ideas they have given or with statements such as "Because I know," thus:

> I think so because I am an American and have and do almost the same things as above. (sixth grade)
> My cerebrum. (seventh grade)
> I am one, I ought to know. (eleventh grade)

TABLE 12-VI

SOURCES FOR CONCEPTS AND ATTITUDES ON MAJORITY
AND MINORITY GROUPS
(Percentage of Children)

	Americans				Negroes				Jews			
	5–6	7–8	9–10	11–12	5–6	7–8	9–10	11–12	5–6	7–8	9–10	11–12
No source, only further elaboration	52	27	29	11	56	31	38	32	64	40	19	34
"I know it to be true"	18	27	27	35	14	15	18	24	4	9	12	18
Historical data, statistics	20	29	31	33	22	16	16	8	4	5	20	2
Personal experience	2	3	8	3	2	6	8	5	8	3	6	5
"People say"	0	2	0	0	0	2	3	3	6	2	4	3
Democratic principles	2	0	1	0	4	10	2	3	0	7	0	0
Parents	2	0	0	3	0	0	0	0	0	2	0	0
School	2	2	0	8	2	0	0	15	0	0	2	3
Books, papers	0	9	7	8	4	32	9	8	0	2	10	3
Movies, radio	0	2	2	3	4	0	1	3	2	0	0	0
Famous persons	0	0	0	0	0	4	2	0	0	2	0	2
Church	0	0	0	0	0	0	0	0	2	0	1	0
"I have no evidence"	0	0	0	0	0	0	1	3	0	0	11	5
Don't know	6	15	3	6	0	0	2	0	0	2	4	0
Omit	0	0	0	0	4	16	13	18	14	34	16	27

A very few children cite personal experience to support their opinions; many cite current happenings or events of history:

> I think that way because the men that brought Negroes over to the country were bringing men and womans to this country just like some people adopt children. (sixth grade)
> Because last year there have been quite a few Negro riots in Detroit and other cities. (tenth grade)

Rarely is a democratic principle given to support a point of view. In cases where a democratic principle is given as a source, the concepts or attitudes toward the minority group are usually accepting ones. Only five children cite the church as a source. In each case the attitude is a positive one:

> Jews are not so bad. I have heard where they give great sums of money to the church. (What makes you think so?) I think so because I have heard our pastor talk about it. (ninth grade)

The children who cite home, school, readings, and movies as sources describe constructive and negative influences.

The Negroes present a great race problem in United States. The South has a hard time controlling the Negroes and their poor habits. (Source) I studied them in social studies. (twelfth grade)

Jews are being treated the worst of any race in Europe. They are often accused of controlling all the big business in the United States but this is not really true because the ratio in business is about the same as the population, about one tenth. (Source) Reading about Jewish problems and oppression and also studying about this in the topic of racial problems in social problems. (twelfth grade)

Negroes are sometimes dishonest and unliked. They are a dirty race and I don't like them. (Source) You can read in the papers about all the killings that have occurred from Negroes. (ninth grade)

Jews get too much of the income of the United States people. They live in joy and comfort. (Source) I think this because it tells it in books and I believe in books. (ninth grade)

I don't know but I wouldn't misjudge them (Jews). I know they're some of our finest business men and are as talented as many of our own race. (Source) I've debated it a lot—with myself. You can't with teachers, it doesn't pay!!!!! (eleventh grade)

The difficulty which the children had in telling the bases for their concepts and attitudes suggests the "unconscious" learning which takes place. It is not likely that concept or attitude is built upon a single vivid learning experience, but rather upon reactions from many sources, in many different settings in the child's daily life—heresay, opinions of others, expressions of derogation, the portrayal of group characteristics in history, fiction, current events, and so forth.

Implications for education would seem to lie in the direction of examining the content of education where cultural diversities can and do play a role, in order to ascertain the nature of influences in this part of the children's experiences.

SUMMARY AND DISCUSSION

Responses were obtained from two hundred and seventy-five school children on the meaning of various American groups. The data reveal a relatively low level of understanding of cultural similarities and differences among people, except in a small proportion of the children. The responses do not indicate either the development of an identification with "American" or with democracy in which idealism or goals of human welfare play a significant role; or the development of social concepts and attitudes which coincide with the "official" or constitutional principles of an American group composed of diverse groups with equal rights and opportunities. These children have assimilated antiminority prejudices through learning which is not based on personal experience with either minority group. The hostile reactions of some of the older children against Negroes and Jews ("Kill them all," "The only good one is a dead one") could not be more violently expressed by the youth of totalitarian indoctrination.

If this sample represents a fair picture of the children of small town midwestern United States, there are many implications for these schools and communities, if their youth is to be made ready and able to live together in a world composed of differences. The children studied show little evidence of constructive teaching from school or church or community which serves to counteract group prejudices. The mere absence of the derogated groups in the community makes teaching of democratic attitudes with respect to them no less necessary. Also, the concept of "American" leaves much to be desired. If it is to serve as a source of personal and group security or as a source of values upon which to build better human relations, it requires a deeper and more significant meaning than "Americans are rugged individualists."

Chapter 13

MATERNAL RESPONSE TO CHILDHOOD AGGRESSION AND SUBSEQUENT ANTI-SEMITISM

DONALD WEATHERLEY

University of Colorado

Two measures of anti-Semitism were obtained from 39 college women. Information concerning maternal handling of their childhood aggression was obtained from their mothers. The results showed that relatively stern maternal discipline toward childhood aggressive behavior was associated with a relatively high level of anti-Semitism in the women.

The role of displaced aggression in the origin and maintenance of ethnic prejudice has been emphasized by a number of theorists[3] and supported in a number of empirical studies.[2,6,8] It is reasonable to assume that individual differences in the readiness to displace aggression onto scapegoats largely originate in childhood, as an outgrowth of parent-child interactions. Particularly pertinent to the scapegoat theory is the manner in which the socialization of aggression is approached by parents. Harsh, restrictive parental handling of childhood aggression is likely to both generate resentment toward authority and foster the development of internal barriers against direct, overt expressions of aggression. Hence the child learns to express his aggression in indirect forms (e.g. prejudice) and against substitute, "safe" objects (e.g. minority group members).

That harsh discipline is a factor in the etiology of ethnic prejudice is suggested by the retrospective accounts of childhood obtained from individuals characterized as authoritarian in orien-

---

Note. Reprinted by permission from *The Journal of Abnormal and Social Psychology, 66* (2):183-185, 1963.

157

tation.[1] Such data, however, are not entirely convincing; the extra punitive tendencies, associated with authoritarianism may well result in systematic distortions in the recollection of childhood treatment. Only two studies known to the author have investigated child rearing information obtained directly from parents of intolerant children.[4,5] Their results support the general principle that rigid, stern discipline is related to the development of prejudice, but these studies bear only incidentally on the question of parental reaction to childhood aggression.

In the present study, data specifically concerning maternal handling of childhood aggression were obtained from mothers of college girls and related to two measures of anti-Semitism obtained from the girls themselves.

METHOD

Thirty-nine non-Jewish undergraduate college women enrolled in elementary psychology courses and their mothers served as subjects.

Daughter Variables

Two measures of anti-Semitism were obtained from the daughters: Levinson Anti-Semitism (A-S) scale scores and scores based on an adaptation of the semantic differential technique.[7] Both scales were administered during regular class periods, the semantic differential approximately five weeks earlier than the A-S scale.

The semantic differential consisted of four names which were to be rated on a list of six seven-step bipolar scales (e.g. good-bad). Four of these bipolar scales, used in the present analysis, consisted of items heavily loaded on the evaluative dimension identified by Osgood and his associates.[7]

Two of the names rated were Jewish-sounding (Samuel Goldblatt and Herbert Rosen); two were non-Jewish (James Brooks and Kenneth Taylor). The names were selected on the basis of their relative "Jewishness" as rated by college students in a previous study.[8] The order of presentation of the four names was systematically varied to control possible order effects.

The sum of each subject's ratings on the seven-step evaluative scales was obtained for the Jewish- and non-Jewish–sounding names. This resulted in scores which reflected the subject's readiness to attribute negative connotations to Jewish- and non-Jewish–sounding names.

Mother Variabes

The mothers were contacted by mail and asked to complete a four-item questionnaire concerning the way in which they reacted to their daughters' aggression in childhood.* Three of the items are pertinent to this study. All were rationally constructed multiple-choice questions.

Two items dealt with the extent to which the mother permitted her daughter to express verbal aggression. One of these items pertained to aggression toward other children, the other to aggression toward parents. The alternatives for each question were weighted in terms of the degree of permissiveness they implied; the average value of the alternatives selected by each mother on these two questions constituted her *permissiveness* score.

The third item concerned the severity of punishment the daughters received for expressing prohibited aggression. A mother's choice of alternatives on this item yielded a *punitiveness* score. Punitiveness and permissiveness scores were unrelated $(r=-.078)$.

Each mother's permissiveness and punitiveness scores were combined to produce a more general index of disciplinary attitudes toward aggression. This was the *sternness* score, obtained by subtracting each mother's permissiveness score from her punitiveness score. Thus high scores on the sternness variable indicated relatively high punitiveness combined with relatively low permissiveness.

Ninety-eight percent of the questionnaires sent to the mothers were completed and returned.

RESULTS AND DISCUSSION

Relationships between mother and daughter variables were assessed by the Pearson r. As can be seen in Table 13-I, the degree of permissiveness reported by mothers was not significantly related

---

*A copy of this questionnaire may be obtained from the author.

TABLE 13-I

CORRELATIONS BETWEEN MEASURES OF MOTHERS' RESPONSES TO
CHILDHOOD AGGRESSION AND DAUGHTERS' ANTI-SEMITISM MEASURES

Mother Variables	Daughter Variables	r
Permissiveness	A-S scale score	—.247
Permissiveness	Jewish name evaluation	—.156
Punitiveness	A-S scale score	+.256
Punitiveness	Jewish name evaluation	+.328*
Sternness	A-S scale score	+.333*
Sternness	Jewish name evaluation	+.338*

Note. N = 39.
*Significant at the .05 level of confidence.

to either index of anti-Semitism obtained from their daughters, although the correlation was negative in both cases.

Maternal punitiveness toward aggressive behavior was positively related to both indices of anti-Semitism obtained from the daughters. In the case of the daughters' evaluation of Jewish-sounding names, the relationship was statistically significant.

The sternness variable, derived from the mothers' permissiveness and punitiveness scores combined, was significantly related to both measures of anti-Semitism. The more stern the maternal discipline toward aggression, the more likely was the daughter to agree with unfavorable statements about Jews on the A-S scale and attribute negative connotations to Jewish-sounding names.

It should be noted that the tendency for the daughters treated relatively punitively and sternly to make more negative evaluations of Jewish-sounding names cannot be interpreted as reflecting a generalized tendency to make negative evaluations. There was no significant relationship found between the daughters' evaluations of non-Jewish-sounding names and the mothers' punitiveness scores ($r = —.065$), sternness scores ($r = +.048$), or permissiveness scores ($r=—.234$).

The findings of this study lend support to the general thesis that important roots of prejudice lie in childhood, in the nature of the parent-child interactions experienced. More specifically, the data fit neatly into a displaced-aggression interpretation of prejudice. Child rearing practices likely to lead to the development of a strong readiness to displace hostility—i.e. relatively punitive, nonpermissive maternal reactions to childhood aggression—are here shown to be related to subsequent anti-Semitism in the children. These results complement other recent findings[2,8] which have shown a relationship between an individual's readiness to displace aggression and his level of prejudice.

Nevertheless, the present data obviously are not decisive evidence for the validity of the scapegoat theory. It may well be, for example, that stern discipline toward childhood aggression is part of a pattern of authoritarian ideology in mothers. Hence it is possible that daughters of relatively stern mothers are more anti-Semitic not primarily because of the way in which they were disciplined for aggressive behavior, but because in identifying with their mothers they have absorbed an authoritarian, anti-Semitic set of attitudes.

REFERENCES

1. ADORNO, T. W., FRENKEL-BRUNSWIK, ELSE, LEVINSON, D. J., and SANFORD, R. N.: *The Authoritarian Personality.* New York, Harper, 1950.
2. BERKOWITZ, L.: Anti-Semitism and the displacement of aggression. *J. Abnorm. Soc. Psychol., 59*:182-187, 1959.
3. DOLLARD, J., DOOB, L. W., MILLER, N. E., MOWRER, O. H., and SEARS, R. R.: *Frustration and Aggression.* New Haven, Yale U. Pr., 1939.
4. FRENKEL-BRUNSWIK, ELSE: A study of prejudice in children. *Hum. Relat., 1*:295-306, 1948.
5. HARRIS, D. B., GOUGH, H. G., and MARTIN, W. E.: Children's ethnic attitudes: II. Relationship to parental beliefs concerning child training. *Child Develop. 21*:169-181, 1950.
6. MILLER, N. E., and BUGELSKI, R.: Minor studies of aggression: II. The influence of frustrations imposed by the in-group on attitudes expressed toward out-groups. *J. Psychol., 25*:437-442, 1948.
7. OSGOOD, C. E., SUCI, G. J., and TANNENBAUM, P. H.: *The Measurement of Meaning.* Urbana, U. Illinois Pr., 1957.
8. WEATHERLEY, D.: Anti-Semitism and the expression of fantasy aggression. *J. Abnorm. Soc. Psychol., 62*:454-457, 1961.

Chapter 14

CHILDREN'S ETHNIC ATTITUDES:
I. RELATIONSHIP TO CERTAIN
PERSONALITY FACTORS

HARRISON G. GOUCH   DALE B. HARRIS
University of California   *University of Minnesota*

AND

WILLIAM E. MARTIN   MARCIA EDWARDS
University of Illinois   *University of Minnesota*

Research on social and ethnic attitudes is lending increasing support to the contention that beliefs and opinions do not exist in isolation and autonomy, but rather are integrated and inter-related in consistent and meaningful fashion. On social issues where attitudes begin to take on an intensity of conviction, where an opinion as to *pro* or *con* commits or obligates the subject in any way, this integrational characteristic is especially marked.

Thus, in the case of pro- or anti-Semitic attitudes an extensive network of related factors has been identified.[3,4] Subjects obtaining high scores on an anti-Semitism scale tend to secure higher scores on various maladjustment inventories, to come from lower socioeconomic environments, to be more categorical in style of thinking, to be less favorably disposed toward other minority groups, toward school, labor unions, and Russia, and to be in favor of universal military training. These relationships are sufficiently strong that ethnic attitudes can be reasonably accurately predicted from knowing how a subject feels about these other issues.[4]

Note. Reprinted by permission from *Child Development,* Vol. 21, No. 2, 1950. This is one of a series of studies on the broad problem of social responsibility being conducted in the Laboratory for Research in Social Relations, University of Minnesota, under a grant from the Carnegie Corporation.

There is reason, too, for believing that this clustering of attitudes and opinions has more than correlational validity. That is, there seems to be a number of underlying variables which synthesize and account for the observed interelationships, such as the fundamental conservatism and ethnocentrism observed by Frenkel-Brunswik and Sanford[3] in their anti-Semitic subjects.

Considerations such as these lead quickly to a concern with developmental questions. If ethnic attitudes are characterized by such a closely knit and fundamental structure in the adult, then it would seem reasonable to suppose that their genesis and early development should be found in the childhood and adolescent years. Frenkel-Brunswik[2] has, indeed, found evidence for such a supposition. In a study of 120 children of ages 11 to 16 who scored at the two extremes of a generalized intolerance scale, the following factors were found to characterize the more prejudiced children: (a) less detached, abstract, and far-reaching sense of social justice, (b) rejection of weakness and individuality, (c) emphasis on dichotomy of sex roles, (d) admiration for strength, power, and money, (e) submission to, but strong resentment of, authority, (f) excessive concern with status values, conventionality, politeness, etc., and external moral values, (g) intolerance for ambiguity, (h) fearful and catastrophic conception of the outside world, and (i) more explosive and diffuse manifestations of aggressiveness.

The purpose of the present study has been to identify some of the correlates of the ethnic attitudes of grade school children with special emphasis on personality factors such as those which have been referred to above. The particular focus has been the attitudes of grade school children toward Negroes.

The Measuring Instruments

The first requirement in carrying out the present study was the construction of a suitable attitude scale which would be meaningful to school children, and which would actually identify children holding more and less favorable opinions concerning Negroes. A large number of measuring devices was considered, but for various reasons, such as complexity of vocabulary, length, inclusion of situations having no experiential relevance for young children, and so forth, none was well suited to our purpose. Because of this it was decided to devise an instrument especially for this study.*

A large number of statements which could pertain to any group, but which included many anti-Negro stereotypes, was written, and from these some 150 which seemed to be simple, unambiguous, and pertinent were selected.

The questions were then given to children in the fifth and sixth grades of a public school, together with a long rectangular card divided into five cells. These cells were inscribed "A very nice thing to say," "A sort of nice thing to say," "Just all right," "A sort of bad thing to say," and "A very bad thing to say." Each child was given a packet of questions, and was then told:

> Each card has a sentence on it. These sentences are things which a child might say about other people. Some of the sentences are nice things to say, some are just all right, and some are bad things to say. You read each sentence and then decide whether you think it is a nice thing to say, or a bad thing to say. After you have decided, place the sentence on the proper pile on the long card in front of you.

The technique here, of course, is the Thurstone judging system for establishing equal-appearing–interval attitude scales.

The children understood the task readily, and had very little difficulty in sorting the questions. An examination of the semi-interquartile ranges for each item permitted the rejection of questions whose valuational connotations were ambiguous or unclear. From this analysis about 75 statements, covering the range from most to least favorable, were retained for the next step.

The next phase in the scale development was the administration of these 75 sentences to third, fourth, and fifth grade students in two different schools. The sentences were presented as a conventional attitude scale, with the instructions that all of the sentences referred to Negroes. The items were read aloud by the examiner, and proctors were present to help any children having trouble in following the instructions, or in understanding the questions.

---

*Dr. Neal Gross of the Department of Sociology of the University of Minnesota, and a member of the Laboratory for Research in Social Relations, collaborated with the authors in developing this scale.

The highest and lowest scoring 25 percent of the papers were chosen, and an item analysis of the entire scale was carried out. This procedure left about 30 sentences which showed good discrimination (at or beyond the 5 percent level in every case), and still covered the total range of reaction. These 30 items were then administered individually to selected children from a third grade class, including good, average, and poor readers, and questions which appeared to be too difficult, or which were responded to on an irrelevant basis, were eliminated. A final scale of 26 items was developed which covered a range of opinion from favorable to unfavorable (as judged by children themselves), which discriminated between high and low scorers, and which could be read and answered sensibly by nearly all of the children at the grade levels selected for study. The split-half reliability of this scale, even in the third grade groups where reading problems would most seriously affect the results, was consistently at or above +.80.

From this 26-item scale (which was used extensively in some of the larger projects mentioned in the opening footnote), 18 most highly differentiating sentences were chosen for the present study. These items, referred to as the "attitude scale," are given below (The instructions specified that all the sentences were about Negroes, and that each was to be answered "agree" or "disagree."):

They work hard.
They make good teachers.
I would like to live next door to them.
I do not like them.
It is easy to be friends with them.
I would like to have them come to eat at my house.
They are good neighbors.
They often hurt other people's feelings.
I would like to be in a club or on a team with them.
They are always honest.
They have done a lot to help our country.
I would not want to ask any of them to a party.
I would like to go on a picnic with them.
They are pretty dumb.
They get excited over little things.
I would like to have one for my teacher next year.
It is a waste of time and money to send them to college.
I would like to see one of them get elected President of the United States.

In addition to this basic scale, "social distance scales" eliciting attitudes toward Negroes, and toward Jews, were also included. The items from the social distance scales are given below:

> I would let them visit our country.
> I would let them live in our country.
> I would let them go to my school.
> I would let them live in my neighborhood.
> I would let them live next door to me.
> I would let them play at my house.
> I would let them come to a party at my house.
> I would let them be my best friends
> I would be willing to marry one of them when I grow up.

A series of eight questions adapted from one of Frenkel-Brunswik's questionnaires was also administered* in order to obtain some direct evidence in the present study on some of the factors she had found in the case of a more general ethnic intolerance. These items, called the "general intolerance scale," are listed below:

> All kinds of people from any race or religion should be allowed to eat in the same restaurant.
> It is a bad thing to have a city divided into different parts with each kind of people living in their own part.
> A dance hall should allow all kinds of people from all races to go to the dance.
> America is a lot better off because of the foreign races that live here.
> The city I live in should allow different kinds of people from different races to stay in the same hotel.
> Different races and religions would get along better if they visited each other and shared things.
> When white people are sick and need blood transfusions, they should be happy to get blood from other races and religions.
> It would be better for everybody if people from all races and nationalities were allowed to go to the same churches.

To the above items 24 personality inventory questions which seemed to embody various factors reported in the literature as related to prejudicial attitudes toward various minority groups were added. Most of the questions were adaptations of personality

---

*The writers wish to thank Dr. Frenkel-Brunswik, and her collaborators, Drs. Milton Rokeach and Murray Jarvik, for making this scale available.

items previously studied,[4] but some were suggested by the papers of Frenkel-Brunswik,[2] and of Frenkel-Brunswik and Sanford.[3] These 24 personality inventory items are reproduced below:

It is all right to get around the law if you don't actually break it.

The most important thing a child can learn is to mind his parents.

The best rule is to play fair with your own gang and let the other children look out for themselves.

About the best way to judge a man's success in life is to see how much money he makes.

If a person is not happy it is just his own fault.

There are only two kinds of people; the weak and the strong.

Teachers should tell the children what to do and not worry about what the children want.

Some day a flood or earthquake will kill everybody in the world.

I think most people would tell a lie to get ahead.

I have often been punished unfairly.

If a person doesn't like the way our country does things he should just keep his mouth shut.

I refuse to play some games because I am not good at them.

Even if a child is being scolded unfairly, he should never talk back to his parents.

I often feel as if I have done something wrong or bad.

Most people are honest only because they are afraid of being caught.

A leader should show that he is the boss and not worry about being nice to people.

Most people will cheat if they can gain something by it.

Most of the other countries of the world are against us, but they are afraid to show it.

Most people hate it when they have to help someone else.

It is really true that you will have bad luck if a black cat crosses your path.

I have more than my share of things to worry about.

It is all right for a person to try and grab everything he can get in this world.

It would be better if the teachers were more strict.

Poor people should look out for themselves and not expect others to help them.

PROCEDURES

The children who were given the tests and questionnaires just described included all those in the fourth, fifth, and sixth grades of two Minneapolis, Minnesota, public schools, giving a total sample of approximately 242 children. From this total, a number of subsamples were picked for special analyses.

The first comparison carried out was between the highest and lowest scoring children on the 18-item attitude scale in each school.* The responses of these children to each of the 24 items in the personality inventory portion of the questionnaire were tabulated; the 13 most significant items emerging from this analysis appear in Table 14-I.

Some readers might question the listing of items with a probability as low as, say, .36 (item 8, school A). The reason for choosing these items for consideration was that the percentage differences were all in the same direction, and the combined probabilities† were less than .05 in all cases.

Inspection of the 13 items in Table 14-I does appear to reveal some of the characteristics which have been found to be associated with prejudice in adolescents and young adults. The more prejudiced child favors his own immediate group over any larger society, he thinks categorically of "weak" and "strong," he declares himself in favor of authoritarianism on the part of the teacher, he is suspicious of the integrity of others, and so forth. In general, the picture one gets of the prejudiced child from this list of statements suggests fear and distrust of others, lack of confidence in self, feelings of guilt and uneasiness, insecurities and doubts about the

---

*The mean score on the 18-item scale for 242 children was 14.0, with a standard deviation of 3.51. A numerically low score indicates existence of prejudice, hence the prejudiced children are more adequately "measured" in this skewed distribution. The estimated reliability of this abbreviated scale by the Kuder-Richardson formula[5] is +.78. This value, although not impressive, is probably satisfactory for an exploratory study.

†The method of combining probabilities is the relationship between the natural logarithm of the probability value and chi-square reported by Palmer O. Johnson, in *Statistical Methods in Research* (N.Y., Prentice Hall, 1949), p. 172, and suggested by him to be applicable to probabilities based on different samples as well as on independent probability estimates on the same sample. The function referred to is $\log_e P = -1/2X^2$, where $d.f. = 2$.

TABLE 14-I

PERSONALITY INVENTORY ITEMS WHICH DISCRIMINATE BETWEEN
CHILDREN WITH HIGH AND LOW SCORES ON THE (NEGRO)
ATTITUDE SCALE IN TWO PUBLIC GRADE SCHOOLS

| Item | School A* Percent Agreement | | | | School B† Percent Agreement | | | |
	Toler-ant	Intol-erant	C.R.	P	Toler-ant	Intol-erant	C.R.	P
1. The best rule is to play fair with your own gang, and let the other children look out for themselves.	40	55	1.31	.20	37	63	2.27	.04
2. There are only two kinds of people: the weak and the strong.	24	61	3.18	.005	34	50	1.41	.18
3. Teachers should tell the children what to do and not worry about what the children want.	26	71	3.92	.001	28	39	1.01	.32
4. I have often been punished unfairly.	24	53	2.60	.01	26	34	0.76	.43
5. If a person doesn't like the way our country does things he should just keep his mouth shut.	37	63	2.35	.03	16	45	2.75	.01
6. I refuse to play some games because I am not good at them.	13	29	1.71	.09	13	39	2.67	.01
7. I often feel as if I had done something wrong or bad.	66	76	0.96	.36	58	84	2.49	.02
8. Most people are honest only because they are afraid of being caught.	29	45	1.35	.18	11	42	3.18	.005
9. Most people will cheat if they can gain something by it.	63	74	1.03	.30	39	66	2.27	.04
10. Most of the other countries of the world are really against us, but are just afraid to show it.	21	58	3.30	.003	16	39	2.33	.03
11. Most people hate it when they have to help someone else.	13	39	2.68	.01	16	37	2.08	.05
12. It is really true that you will have bad luck if a black cat crosses your path.	5	18	1.78	.08	0	8	1.78	.08
13. I have more than my share of things to worry about.	24	42	1.67	.10	16	39	2.33	.03

*The two samples from this school each consisted of 20 boys and 18 girls.
†The two samples from this school each consisted of 19 boys and 19 girls.

larger physical and social world, and possibly a reactive hostility toward people who are "weak" or "different."

A similar analysis of the 24 personality items was carried out using the eight general intolerance questions adapted from the Frenkel-Brunswik scale as a criterion. Only six personality items were retained in this analysis. Two of these items, nos. 3 and 5 in Table 14-II, fell above the 5 percent level but below the 10 percent level by the combined probability criterion. This small number of items probably reflects the unreliability of the criterion measure more than an actual lack of association. Scores on the general intolerance scale could only vary from zero to eight, which necessitated a marked reduction of the actual range of opinion which could be assumed to exist. The items which emerged in this analysis are presented in Table 14-II.

Although the levels of significance are distinctly lower in this analysis than in the previous one, the same kinds of factors seem

TABLE 14-II

PERSONALITY INVENTORY ITEMS WHICH DISCRIMINATE BETWEEN CHILDREN WITH HIGH AND LOW SCORES ON THE GENERAL INTOLERANCE SCALE IN TWO PUBLIC GRADE SCHOOLS

| | School A* Percent Agreement | | | | School B† Percent Agreement | | | |
Item	Toler-ant	Intol-erant	C.R.	P	Toler-ant	Intol-erant	C.R.	P
1. It is all right to get around the law if you don't actually break it.	54	68	1.08	.28	47	68	1.85	.06
2. The best rule is to play fair with your own gang, and let the other children look out for themselves.	36	61	1.87	.07	50	63	1.14	.24
3. There are only two kinds of people: the weak and the strong.	39	46	0.53	.62	29	53	2.13	.03
4. I refuse to play some games because I am not good at them.	18	36	1.52	.14	13	29	1.81	.07
5. It is really true that you will have bad luck if a black cat crosses your path.	7	25	1.83	.08	5	8	0.53	.57
6. I have more than my share of things to worry about.	21	54	2.55	.02	21	34	1.27	.20

*The two samples from this school each consisted of 14 boys and 14 girls.
†The two samples from this school each consisted of 19 boys and 19 girls.

also to characterize the less tolerant children when selected according to scores on this shorter, more generalized, attitude scale.

The final item analysis of the 24 personality questions was in relation to the social distance scale concerning Jews. The distribution of scores on the social distance scale showed the same attenuation found for the general intolerance scale, and in addition a noticeable clustering of scores near the most accepting end of the continuum. These facts made it difficult to obtain pairs of samples clearly differentiated by their responses on the social distance scale. The samples chosen, as indicated in Table 14-III, were quite small.

In Table 14-III it appears again that, although the retained items are not as clearly significant as in Table 14-I, the general pattern of response is similar. The less tolerant children, as judged by the social distance scale, have a cynical, distrustful opinion of

TABLE 14-III

PERSONALITY INVENTORY ITEMS WHICH DISCRIMINATE BETWEEN CHILDREN WITH HIGH AND LOW SCORES ON THE SOCIAL DISTANCE SCALE (TOWARD JEWS) IN TWO PUBLIC GRADE SCHOOLS

Item	School A* Percent Agreement				School B† Percent Agreement			
	Toler-ant	Intol-erant	C.R.	P	Toler-ant	Intol-erant	C.R.	P
1. If a person is not happy it is just his own fault.	31	63	1.76	.10	28	56	2.01	.06
2. I think most people would tell a lie to get ahead.	37	50	0.68	.45	36	64	1.98	.06
3. Most people are honest only because they are afraid of being caught.	19	25	0.41	.70	8	40	2.65	.03
4. Most people will cheat if they can gain something by it.	56	63	0.34	.75	52	84	2.43	.02
5. Most of the other countries of the world are against us, but are just afraid to show it.	18	50	1.84	.08	16	52	2.69	.015
6. Most people hate it when they have to help someone else.	25	37	0.79	.44	16	48	2.43	.02
7. I have more than my share of things to worry about.	19	69	2.85	.01	12	48	2.78	.01

*The two samples from this school each consisted of 8 boys and 8 girls.
†The two samples from this school each consisted of 9 boys and 16 girls.

others, are fearful of being exploited or duped, or have feelings of having been treated unfairly.

SUMMARY

If we attempt to synthesize briefly the materials reported in this paper, it would appear that the following conclusions are justified:

1. There is a relationship between children's attitudes toward specific groups, such as Negroes and Jews, and between such attitudes and scales assessing more generalized reactions of tolerance and intolerance.

2. Responses to personality inventory items which embody sentiments of hostility, resentment, distrust, insecurity, and so on can be shown to be related to both the more particular, and more generalized, attitudes mentioned above; moreover, the direction of relationship is the same in all cases.

3. School children, then, who appear to be more intolerant also give evidence of being more constricted, cynical, and fearful, less confident and secure, and more suspicious and more ethnocentric than children of greater tolerance.

Such results suggest that to bring about real and lasting changes in social attitudes one must attend to the total personality structure as well as specific attitudes. Possibly this structure provides one of the basic conditions under which attitudes, desirable or undesirable, originate, develop, and flourish. It would seem reasonable to expect that, as long as a given personality system persists, clusters of attitudes which are consistent with that system will also persist. Changes in attitudes may then, to a large extent, be dependent upon changes in the total personality. Programs of social welfare and amelioration should take account of considerations such as these if the goals include an initiation of stable and meaningful changes in attitudes and perspectives.

REFERENCES

1. FRENKEL-BRUNSWIK, ELSE: Dynamic and cognitive categorization of qualitative material: II. Application to interviews with the ethnically prejudiced. *J. Psychol.*, 25:261-277, 1948.

2. FRENKEL-BRUNSWIK, ELSE: A study of prejudice in children. *Hum. Relat., 1*:295-306, 1948.
3. FRENKEL-BRUNSWIK, ELSE, and SANFORD, R. N.: Some personality factors in anti-Semitism. *J. Psychol., 20*:271-291, 1945.
4. GOUGH, H. G.: *Personality Correlates of Social and Ethnic Attitudes among High School Students.* Ph.D. dissertation. Minneapolis, University of Minnesota, 1949.
5. KUDER, G. F., and RICHARDSON, M. W.: The theory of the estimation of test reliability. *Psychometrika, 2*:151-160, 1937.

IV. MODIFICATION OF PREJUDICE

The need is not really for more brains;
The need is now for a gentler, more tolerant people than
    those who won for us against the ice, the tiger and the
    bear.
The hand that hefted the ax, out of some blind allegiance to
    the past, fondles the machine gun as lovingly.
It is a habit man will have to break to survive. But the roots
    go very deep.

—LOREN EISELEY

Chapter 15

THE DIFFERENTIAL NATURE OF PREJUDICE REDUCTION

JOHN H. MANN
New York University

PROBLEM

One of the problems which has concerned social scientists during the last few decades is how to devise means by which racial prejudice can be reduced. Studies in this area have typically involved testing the effectiveness of particular methods which are purported to reduce racial prejudice using whatever criteria seemed appropriate to the investigator. These studies have recently been summarized by Allport,[2] Saenger,[7] and Harding, Kutner, Prohansky, and Chein.[5] The latter authors have emphasized the importance of measuring racial prejudice in terms of affective, cognitive, and conative components, and specifying the effect of a given change procedure on each component. In this connection they state that it is necessary to examine "the functional dependence of intergroup attitudinal components on each other. Do changes in any one of them necessarily imply corresponding changes in the others? There is very little direct evidence on this point"[5] (p 1030).

The problem of the functional dependence of components of racial prejudice has both practical and theoretical importance. From a practical viewpoint it is necessary to know whether one can change the most tractable aspect of racial prejudice and assume that other aspects will show an equivalent change. If this is the case the practitioner's task is simplified. If this is not the case,

Note. Reprinted by permission from *The Journal of Social Psychology, 52:339-343*, 1960. Based on a paper presented at the 1958 convention of the American Psychological Association.

however, the practitioner must consider the possibility of having to change each component of racial prejudice by a different means.

From a theoretical viewpoint the degree of functional dependence between the components of racial prejudice has direct implications for a general theory of personality change. Racial prejudice may be viewed as a sample personality attitude. To the extent that this is the case the functional dependence between the cognitive, affective, and behavioral aspects of this attitude may be representative of the functional dependence of these components in other attitudes and aspects of personality.

With these considerations in mind the present study was undertaken in order to determine whether change in one component of racial prejudice is reflected by parallel changes in other components.

METHOD

In order to determine whether cognitive, affective, and behavioral aspects of racial prejudice are functionally related, measures of these variables were obtained from the members of several small interracial groups near the beginning and near the end of their small-group experience.

The experimental subjects were members of a graduate course in education. Forty-seven of the subjects were white and 31 were Negro. Thirty of the white subjects were Protestant and 17 were Catholic. Thirty of the Negro subjects were Protestant and one was Catholic. Thirty-four of the subjects were males and 44 were female. Forty-two of the subjects lived in the North and 36 lived in the South. The median age of the subjects was 30. The age range extended from 22 to 60 years.

The subjects were assigned to six-man groups by a system of random numbers. Thirteen such groups were formed, consisting of a total of 78 persons. Group members were not previously acquainted with each other. Each group met in leaderless group discussion four times a week over a three-week period. Each meeting varied in length from one hour to one hour and a half. These leaderless groups were an integral part of the graduate course in which all subjects were enrolled. The course emphasized the importance of democratic sharing of ideas, feelings, and experiences.

The groups were designed to provide a setting for such a democratic sharing. They therefore provided a setting for interracial group contact characterized by the elements which Allport[2] has described as tending to reduce racial prejudice, namely, equal status, institutional sanction, and common goals (as defined by the course content). The conditions were, therefore, such as to encourage prejudice reduction in one or more of the components of racial prejudice.

Instruments

Three instruments were used in order to measure change in the cognitive, affective, and behavioral aspects of racial prejudice. The E scale from the California Public Opinion Survey was used in order to obtain a measure of the cognitive aspects of racial prejudice. Only the "patriotism" subscale of the total E scale was used in order to increase the speed with which the E scale could be administered. This subscale is reported by Levinson[1] to have a correlation of .92 with the total E scale. A split-half reliability check of the subscale yielded a coefficient of .78 which compared favorably with the split-half reliability of .80 reported by Levinson.[1]

A sociometric questionnaire was used in order to obtain a measure of the affective aspect of racial prejudice. This questionnaire required that the individual rank order the group on the criterion "Whom would you most like to continue to be friends with at the end of the summer session?" This questionnaire was adapted from Ausubel.[3] Since Ausubel, Schiff, and Gasser[4] found that the sociometric choices of subjects using the questionnaire were positively skewed, a forced choice procedure was introduced into the questionnaire used in the present study in order to correct for this tendency.

In order to obtain a measure of the behavioral aspect of racial prejudice each group member was asked to rank other group members on the criterion "amount of racial prejudice." It was assumed that when group members ranked each other on this criterion, they were responding to the behavior or behavioral tendencies which they observed in other group members.

All of these instruments were administered to all experimental subjects at the third and eleventh general class sessions of the graduate course which they were all attending.

RESULTS

In order to be able to test the degree of functional dependence which existed among the components of racial prejudice, it was necessary to establish that at least one of these components had undergone a significant change during the course of the small-group experience. A comparison was therefore made of the early and late E scale scores by the use of a Mann-Whitney U-test. A critical ratio of 2.67 was obtained indicating that the cognitive aspect of prejudice had been reduced.

Pre-post difference scores were then derived for each measure of prejudice for all 78 subjects. These difference scores were correlated with each other in order to determine whether the three components of prejudice were, in fact, functionally dependent. A correlation of —.12 was obtained between the cognitive and affective pre-post difference scores. A correlation of .09 was obtained between the cognitive and behavioral pre-post difference scores. Finally a correlation —.05 was obtained between the behavioral and affective pre-post difference scores. None of these correlations are significant. The results of this study indicate, therefore, that there is no functional dependence among the cognitive, affective, and behavioral components of racial prejudice.

DISCUSSION

The findings of the study are negative. The reliability of the measuring instruments must therefore be considered, since lack of findings may be due to low reliability rather than lack of relationship. The E scale was reported earlier to have a split-half reliability of .78. Ausubel reports a corrected split-half reliability for the sociometric questionnaire on which the present sociometric questionnaire is based of .90. The reliability of the group members' prejudice ranking has not been determined. However in a previous study[6] the author found that this measure correlated as high as .54 with other measures, indicating that the measure must have reasonable reliability. The evidence would seem to indicate, therefore, that the lack of positive findings cannot be attributed to the unreliability of the measuring instruments.

For the practitioner interested in the reduction of racial prejudice these findings suggest a pessimistic but important conclusion, namely that each component of racial prejudice must be reduced separately since change in one component is unrelated to change in other components. This conclusion suggests the importance of determining the differential effectiveness of various prejudice-reducing techniques on the various components of racial prejudice. It seems reasonable to assume that different techniques influence different components. If this proves to be the case it would be important for the practitioner to give increased emphasis to accurate differential diagnosis of the relative contribution of the various components of racial prejudice in any given situation and base his choice of remedial technique upon the results of such a diagnosis.

From the theoretical point of view the findings suggest a three-factor approach to the change process. It has often been customary to view personality and attitudinal change as a global process in which the whole personality is reorganized or reconstituted. The present findings suggest that differential changes in cognitive, affective, and behavioral components of an aspect of personality are possible. This finding has important implications for a general theory of personality change and deserves to be replicated on other aspects of personality.

SUMMARY

This study considered the functional dependence of the cognitive, affective, and behavioral components of racial prejudice. The subjects of this inquiry were 78 students participating in a graduate course in education. Each subject was randomly assigned to a six-man group. These groups met in leaderless group discussion four times a week over a three-week period. During the first and third week three questionnaires which measured cognitive, affective, and behavioral aspects of racial prejudice were given to all subjects. Pre-post difference scores were computed for each subject on each measure and these difference scores were intercorrelated. The results of this analysis indicated that (a) the cognitive measure of prejudice decreased significantly during the course of the group experience, and (b) there was no functional dependence between cognitive, affective, and behavioral components of racial prejudice.

REFERENCES

1. ADORNO, T. W., FRENKEL-BRUNSWIK, E., LEVINSON, D. J., and SANFORD, R. N.: *The Authoritarian Personality.* New York, Harper, 1950.
2. ALLPORT, G. W.: *The Nature of Prejudice.* Cambridge, Addison-Wesley, 1954.
3. AUSUBEL, D. P.: Reciprocity and assumed reciprocity of acceptance among adolescents, a sociometric study. *Sociometry, 16:* 339-348, 1953.
4. AUSUBEL, D. P., SCHIFF, H. N., and GASSER, E. B.: A preliminary study of developmental trends in sociempathy: accuracy of perception of own and others' sociometric status. *Child Develop., 23:*111-128, 1952.
5. HARDING, J., KUTNER, B., PROHANSKY, H., and CHEIN, I.: Prejudice and ethnic relations. In G. Lindzey (Ed.): *Handbook of Social Psychology.* Cambridge, Addison-Wesley, 1954, p. 1021-1061.
6. MANN, J. H.: Influence of racial prejudice on sociometric status in inter-racial groups. *Psychol. Rep., 3:*585-588, 1957.
7. SAENGER, G.: *The Social Psychology of Prejudice.* New York, Harper, 1953.

Chapter 16

MODIFYING PREJUDICE: ATTITUDE CHANGE AS A FUNCTION OF THE RACE OF THE COMMUNICATOR

SIDNEY KRAUS

Indiana University

The gifted communicator takes into account the fact that his audience's feelings toward him can impede or increase his persuasiveness. Hovland and coauthors[6] have briefly but adequately outlined the relationship of these feelings toward the communicator as follows:

> We shall assume that . . . various effects of the communicator are mediated by attitudes toward him which are held by members of the audience. Any number of different attitudes may underlie the influence exerted by a given communicator. Some may have to do with feelings of affection and admiration, and stem in part from desires to be like him. Others may involve awe and fear of the communicator, based on perceptions of his power to reward or punish according to one's adherence to his recommendations or demands. Still other important attitudes are those of trust and confidence. These are related to perceptions of the communicator's credibility, including beliefs about his knowledge, intelligence, and sincerity.

The attitudes this quotation summarizes are brought about through the manifestation of certain emotional and psychological characteristics of the communicator. While these characteristics are admittedly important, what of the physical characteristics which the communicator exhibits? This is an important variable in visual communication, especially in television.

Note. Reprinted by permission from *Audiovisual Communication Review,* 10(1): 14-22, 1960. The author wishes to acknowledge the encouragement of Paul J. Heinberg and Samuel L. Becker, Department of Speech and Theater, State University of Iowa.

183

The study reported here was undertaken to investigate just one such physical characteristic, that of race. More specifically, the study was concerned with the relative effectiveness of Negro and white actors in changing the attitudes of 11th grade white children toward Negroes.

Previous Research

There have been many studies in which different variables have been investigated to determine their effect(s) in changing attitudes. Williams[24] reported that children's participation in dramatization was the most effective teaching method for changing their attitudes toward Negroes; their viewing of motion pictures was second; their listening to material read by the teacher was least effective. Willis,[25] using the radio medium, found that dramatization proved more effective than either "straight talk" or a combination of the two methods in changing various attitudes.

Concerning the effect of content on attitude change, Rosenthal,[16] Wiese and Cole,[23] and Ramseyer[14] all showed that the attitudes which were changed were those most directly related to film content. Thurstone and Peterson[22] provided some indication that the bias of film content should also be in the direction of the attitude to be influenced.

Psychological analysis of behavior and the background of a given situation—when explained to an audience—can help to change attitudes. Rubin-Rabsom[17] found that lectures explaining personality dynamics helped bring about a change of attitude toward criminality. Schlorff[18] and Links[9] both effected changes in racial attitudes. Links' conclusion[9] (p 46) was similar to that of Schlorff's experiment. She said:

> Significance of race-attitude change tends to be related to the extent and thoroughness with which facts about a people are presented in an integrated combination with information about the personal and psychological motives, resources and feelings of the people, placed in an accurate historic perspective.

Most important to the experiment reported here, perhaps, is the factor of audience involvement with the presentation. Kishler,[7] who studied the main character in a film, stated:

. . . a knowledge of an intended audience's identifications with [positive attitudes toward] persons and groups, can give major clues concerning the characteristics that should be exhibited by the main character of a motion picture in order to facilitate learning of the information and acceptance of the ideas presented in the motion picture.

Hoban and Van Ormer[4] state:

. . . the ability of any medium of communication . . . to modify motivations, attitudes, and opinions lies not so much in the medium itself, but in the relationship of content and bias of the medium to (a) the personality structure of the perceiving individuals, and (b) the social environment of the audience.

Scollon[19] found that for a film to be most effective in changing attitudes, the communicator should be well characterized as a figure of prestige, and highly related to the audience reference group.

Maccoby and Wilson[10] (p 86) demonstrated that viewers of a film tended to identify themselves with a character in the social class to which they aspired rather than with one in their own class. This finding was evidenced even more by males than by females. In addition, the researchers concluded: "Memory for movie content appears to be influenced *both* by identification with a character in the movie and by the need-relevance of a particular kind of content for the viewer." Mertens also found that for attitude-change, material should relate to needs of the audience.

Rath and Trager[15] and Cooper and Dinerman[2] both showed previously produced films* to high school audiences in an effort to reduce prejudice toward ethnic groups. Rath and Trager found no change in the viewers' basic attitudes. The results of the Cooper and Dinerman study showed "some effect on specific messages," but no effect on general messages.

The previous research here cited provides some indication that (1) specificity and bias of material should be directed toward the attitude to be changed; (2) psychological analysis of behavior, and the background of a given situation, should be included in

---

*Some researchers have pointed out that films especially planned and produced for comparison with each other are more efficient for objective study than films that have already been produced.[5]

the material; (3) identification can be important if attitudes are to be modified; and (4) prestige of the communicator is influential in restructuring attitudes. The writer utilized these four factors in his study as criteria for structuring the stimulus, a kinescope recording.

The experiment, then, proposed to examine the relative effectiveness of such a kinescope in changing attitudes toward Negroes with the independent variable being the race of the actions involved.

PROCEDURE

In this study, the following questions were investigated: (1) Can a recorded television presentation structured on the findings of previous research modify the attitudes of eleventh grade white students in a favorable direction toward Negroes and their integration in education? (2) Can white performers in such a film effect greater attitude modification than Negro performers, or vice versa, or should the cast be white and Negro?

To attempt to answer the above questions, the first step was to write an original script about the efforts of two high school teachers to secure admittance of a Negro student to a white private college. Four 11-minute kinescope recordings were produced with identical dialogue which differed in all respects as little as possible, except in terms of the performers. Version I used two white performers; version 2, two Negro performers; version 3, one white performer and one Negro performer; and version 4, the same as 3, but with the roles reversed.

A panel of 30 instructors and students matched the performers as much as possible in terms of height, general appearance, and acting ability. Two competent Negro performers were available at the time of this phase of the study. Their names were placed in separate columns on a sheet of paper distributed to the panel. Under each of their names the names of the same eight white potential performers were listed. The group was asked to rank each name as a white "counterpart" of the Negro name listed above.

The sample population for this experiment was obtained from Iowa high schools in towns of less than 7,000 population, with 525 eleventh grade students in nine schools in the experimental design. The towns were selected from those geographically located near Iowa City. Eight of the schools were assigned in pairs for exposure to one of the four treatments. The ninth school, largest in number of students, was used as a control.

Attitude Scale

To measure the attitudes of the subjects toward concepts relevant to the content of the film, an attitude test was constructed and refined. This test is referred to in this article as the "attitude scale." Attitude change, therefore, is the difference in score between a test administered to the students five weeks before they viewed the films (pretest), and the same test administered immediately after they viewed the film (posttest). For additional information of potential future use, the Negro subscale of the California Ethnocentric Attitude Scale[1]—hereafter referred to as the "California *E*"—was administered with the "attitude scale."

As a precaution against a possible cuing effect, 25 subjects from only one school in each of the four treatment groups were pretested. Five weeks after pretesting, all eight groups were posttested immediately after they viewed the film. The control group, pretested prior to the others groups, was posttested after the other groups. Statistical analyses were made of the data to test the following null hypotheses: (a) the films did not significantly change attitudes; (b) no version was significantly different from the others in changing attitudes.

The attitude scale employed was identical in format to those employed by Osgood, Suci, and Tannenbaum.[12] Each concept is rated on a seven-interval bipolar scale. At the poles are adjectival opposites. For example, the concept "Negro" may be judged against the scale, good—:—:—:—:—:—:—bad. Three basic factors have been identified in this type of scaling. They are labeled as (a) *evaluative*, (b) *potency*, and (c) *activity*. Osgood and Tannenbaum[13] have shown that the first factor, *evaluative*—characterized by such adjectival opposites as *valuable-worthless, good-bad,* and so forth—is similar to the basic attitudinal continuum which other attitude-measurement techniques index. Osgood, Suci, and Tannenbaum further state that they believe a quantitative measurement of meaning in a multidimensional semantic space can be obtained.

The attitude scale for this study does not attempt to locate that semantic space. However, the technique developed as already described was utilized in this experiment. The writer believed that only the *evaluative* scales would provide a valid measure of attitude. As Tannebaum[21] states this view:

> Attitude toward a concept is . . . defined as the allocation of the concept of the evaluative dimension of meaning. More operationally, attitude is the rating of that concept on scales that represent the evaluative dimension.

This study adapts Tannenbaum's operational definition of attitude to the attitude scale with the understanding that the scales' *dimension* in terms of meaning is not the concern of this study.

Suci[20] found that the *evaluative* scales* for judgments of ethnic group labels correlated highly with scores on the California *E*. Partly because of this finding and in order to select the concepts to be used in the final attitude scale, the writer randomly selected 30 married students' wives for an initial testing of the concepts and their correlation with the California *E*.

Negro Subscale

Contrary to Suci's finding, the correlation obtained in this preliminary testing between the attitude scale and the California *E* ($r=.13$) was such that the researcher decided to utilize only those items included in the Negro subscale of the California *E*. Five concepts—"Negro leaders," "Negro neighbors," "Negro principal," "integration" and "Negro students"*—whose correlations were highest (r ranging from .16 to .50; standard error $= .19$) were employed in the final attitude scale.

---

*Scales used in the present study: *fair-unfair, clean-dirty, like-dislike, good-bad, pleasant-unpleasant, valuable-worthless, intelligent-unintelligent.*

*Subjects were instructed to respond to these concepts with regard to each of the scales; *e.g. Negro neighbors:* good-bad.

ANALYSIS OF THE DATA

Scoring

The attitude scale was scored by assigning each of the seven steps a value from one to seven. The favorable pole of the scale was scored as one, and the unfavorable pole was scored as seven.

The attitude score for a particular concept was obtained by a summation of the scores on the seven *evaluative* scales. These concept totals were summed to give a total score for a subject. There were five concepts and seven scales. Hence, the highest possible score was 245; the lowest possible was 35. A low score would be an indication of less prejudice, while a high score would indicate more prejudice.

When raw scores were converted to positive integers, the highest possible score on the California E was 36 and the lowest possible score was six. Here again, since the statements were prejudicial in nature, a low score indicates less prejudice.

The same scoring system was followed for both the pretest and posttest. By a comparison of pretest and posttest means for any group, a measure of shift in attitude of that group was obtained.

Analysis

Pretest data were processed to determine the intercorrelations of the California E with each scale and concept. It was predetermined that those scales and the concepts with the highest correlations would be included in the final analysis.

The following analyses were conducted separately for the attitude scale and for the California E: (a) Pretest data were submitted to analysis of variance and t-tests to determine whether or not the groups were nonheterogeneous. If a group was found to be heterogeneous, it was eliminated from further analysis. (b) Analysis of variance and t-tests were used to determine nonheterogeneity of those groups which were not pretested. This was done by comparing the posttest data within treatments. (c) By the application of t-tests to the posttests of groups *within* treatments, it was possible to combine into *one group* those groups which viewed the same film. (d) Hence, the combined posttests (the *one group*) was compared with the pretest in the same treatment to obtain a measure of attitude shift. Analysis of variance and *t*-tests were used in this phase of the procedure. (e) A simple analysis of variance was applied for an overall *F*-test to test the null hypotheses;[8] *t*-tests were applied where significance indicated.

RESULTS

Attitude Scale

For final analysis, groups were combined into *one audience; i.e.* those schools in which students viewed the same kinescope and which were nonheterogeneous were treated as one group in the analysis.

Reliability of ratings for all subjects was computed by adapting Ebel's formula.[3] A high reliability of .97 was found.

In order to test for significance in shift of attitude (from pretest to posttest), a *t*-test for each concept, using total concept mean score in each version, was computed. The results can be seen in Table 16-I.

Only two concepts in one version proved to be significant ($p < .05$)—"Negro neighbors" and "integration" in version 4. In both instances, the mean of the posttest was significantly less than

TABLE 16-I

T-TEST TO DETERMINE SIGNIFICANT SHIFT IN ATTITUDE
ON CONCEPTS IN EACH VERSION

Version and Concept	Pretest M	S.D.	Posttest M	S.D.	Degrees of Freedom	t	Sig.
1—White Performers					38		
Negro neighbors	18.20	8.36	20.85	9.16		.93	NS
Integration	18.85	10.04	21.10	9.42		.72	NS
Negro principal	24.00	9.22	24.65	10.18		.21	NS
Negro leaders	22.55	10.69	22.90	10.82		.10	NS
Negro students	16.75	7.71	20.60	8.85		1.43	NS
2—Negro Performers					69		
Negro neighbors	18.50	5.86	21.41	8.36		1.46	NS
Integration	16.95	6.15	19.59	8.96		1.24	NS
Negro principal	22.86	7.84	21.29	8.79		.71	NS
Negro leaders	19.95	8.17	21.31	9.42		.58	NS
Negro students	16.36	5.69	18.55	8.95		1.04	NS
4—White and Negro Performers					81		
Negro neighbors	19.30	6.50	15.96	6.28		2.21	S
Integration	20.61	9.68	14.64	7.16		3.21	S
Negro principal	21.13	9.09	17.35	8.08		1.91	NS
Negro leaders	20.04	10.15	17.85	9.30		.96	NS
Negro students	16.83	7.09	14.72	7.53		1.19	NS

the mean of the pretest; thus, on these concepts, subjects in version 4 (with reversal of roles in 3) became significantly less prejudiced toward the Negro than they were prior to their viewing of the kinescope.

That kinescope 4 was significantly better in reducing prejudice than the other kinescopes, or than no kinescope, was supported by analysis of variance $(F=5.73; p<.01)$ and subsequent t-tests. Table 16-II shows that version 4 was significantly superior to the other kinescopes in shifting attitude scores in a favorable direction toward Negroes.

Using the total score of each concept as the criterion measure, the writer then utilized analysis of variance to determine the relative effectiveness of the kinescopes for each concept. Again, statistical evidence supports kinescope 4, presenting one white performer and one Negro performer. All concepts except "Negro leaders" were significant.

California E

In the final analysis of the California E, there were no statistically significant differences. With use of Ebel's formula, the reliability for all subjects' responses on the California E was found to be .94. The correlation between the attitude scale and the California E, using the data from the final analysis, was .63.*

TABLE 16-II

T TABLE OF DIFFERENCE BETWEEN VERSION MEANS FOR WHICH
SIGNIFICANT EFFECT WAS FOUND IN ANALYSIS OF
VARIANCE ATTITUDE SCALE

Versions*	M_1	$S.D._1$	M_2	$S.D._2$	df.	t	Sig.
1—2	109.60	7.17	102.14	4.02	67	.74	NS
1—4	109.60	7.17	80.54	3.01	99	3.07	S
1—Control	109.60	7.17	98.51	4.17	112	1.19	NS
2—4	102.14	4.02	80.54	3.01	128	3.15	S
2—Control	102.14	4.02	98.51	4.17	141	.60	NS
4—Control	80.54	3.01	98.51	4.17	173	3.14	S

*1 = white performers; 2 = Negro performers; 4 = white and Negro performers; Control = no kinescope.

*A high correlation was found between the attitude scale and the California E, and both tests were found to be highly reliable for all subjects. The California E consistently agreed with the results of the attitude scale, but was not as discriminating. Hence, both seem to measure much the same thing $(r = .63)$ but the attitude scale measured more precisely.

Version 3 Kinescope

Because of the heterogeneity of variance on the initial measures, the subjects who viewed the kinescope in version 3 were
eliminated from analysis with the other groups. However, since
version 4 (with reversal of roles in 3) was found to be significant,
the researcher decided that a separate analysis should be conducted.
T-tests revealed that responses to three concepts—"Negro neighbors," "integration," "Negro principal"—were significant ($p<.05$).

Analysis of Covariance

Those students in each treatment who completed both the
pretest and the posttest on the attitude scale ($N=88$) were included in the analysis of covariance to determine which kinescope
differed—and subsequently was better—in reducing prejudice. This
analysis was conducted for a more rigid test of the data.

The analysis revealed an *F* of 4.92, ($p<.01$). Results of *t*-tests
to determine which films were better than other films in reducing
prejudice are shown in Table 16-III. In summary they were as
follows:

1. Versions 3 and 4 were significantly better than version 1,
and version 3 was significantly better than version 2.
2. Version 1 did not differ significantly from version 2.
3. Version 2 did not differ significantly from version 4.
4. Version 3 did not differ significantly from version 4.

The same analysis was conducted for the California *E* using the
same subjects ($N=88$). No significance was found at $p=.05$.

TABLE 16-III
T TABLE OF DIFFERENCES BETWEEN VERSION MEANS FOR WHICH
SIGNIFICANT EFFECT WAS FOUND IN ANALYSIS OF
COVARIANCE ATTITUDE SCALE

Vesions*	M_1	M_2	*t*	*Sig.*
1—2	101.72	90.24	1.13	NS
1—3	101.72	75.38	3.56	S
1—4	101.72	81.36	2.88	S
2—3	90.24	75.38	2.09	S
2—4	90.24	81.36	1.29	NS
3—4	75.38	81.36	.84	NS

*1 = white performers; 2 = Negro performers; 3 = white and Negro performers;
4 = reversal of roles in 3.

The results of these two analyses agree, for the most part, with the analyses conducted in the primary study.

CONCLUSIONS

Versions 3 and 4 were the films which significantly changed attitudes. Each of these films included one white performer and one Negro performer; these persons' roles were reversed in version 4. Although it is true that version 3 could not be compared directly with the other versions, a separate analysis provided evidence that version 3 was significant. When considering that, in effect, each of the four versions was tested separately (*t*-tests within treatments), and only versions 3 and 4 proved to be significant, it can be concluded that both of these versions are significantly better in changing attitudes than are versions 1 and 2. Hence, it follows that since the roles in 3 and 4 were reversed, the roles as such were not a factor in the significance found.

The findings in this study seem to indicate that eleventh grade white students are more convinced as to the sincerity of the communicator (the performer) when he is practicing what he preaches, or, to use another cliché, when action speaks louder than words. When such students see two white individuals preaching about the rights of Negroes, or when they see two Negroes in a similar discussion, they tend to withdraw from the appeal being made. However, when they see a white person talking about the rights of Negroes in a favorable context to a Negro with whom he shares certain cultural values and norms, they are impressed with the sincerity of the communicator. The students identify themselves with the communicator—they have shared experiences, and moreover, are able to share understanding—that is, they empathized. They thus modify their previously held attitudes.

It would be interesting to test whether results of this study can be generalized beyond prejudice toward Negroes, or beyond physical characteristics; *e.g.* if one wanted to change the attitudes of individuals toward capital punishment, would it be more effective to have as performers two actors not sentenced to die, two actors sentenced to die, *or one of each?*

Additional experimental research testing the interaction be-

tween the physical characteristics of the communicator and the
ideas he presents should help to further our knowledge about communicator variables with regard to change of attitude.

REFERENCES

1. ADORNO, T. W., et al.: *The Authoritarian Personality.* New York,
   Harper and Bros., 1950, pp. 104-50.
2. COOPER, S., and DINERMAN, H.: An analysis of the film "Don't be
   a Sucker": A study in comumnication. *Public Opinion Quarterly, 15*:243-64, 1951.
3. EBEL, R. L.: Estimation of the reliability of ratings. *Psychometrika, 16*:407-24, 1951.
4. HOBAN, CHARLES F., and VAN ORMER, EDWARD B.: *Instructional
   Film Research 1918-1950.* Technical Report SDC 269-7-19. Port
   Washington, Long Island, New York, Special Devices Center,
   Office of Naval Resarch, 1951, pp. 5-20.
5. HOVLAND, C. J., LUMSDAINE, A. A., and SHEFFIELD, F. D. *Experiments on Mass Communication. Studies in Social Psychology
   in World War II.* Princeton, Princeton U. Pr., 1949, vol. 3.
6. HOVLAND, C. J., JANIS, I. L., and KELLEY, H. H.: *Communication
   and Persuasion.* New Haven, Yale U. Pr., 1953, p. 20.
7. KISHLER, JOHN P.: *The Effects of Prestige and Identification Factors on Attitude Restructuring and Learning from Sound
   Films.* Technical Report SDC 269-7-10. Washington, D. C.,
   Dept. of Commerce, Office of Technical Services, 1950, p. 11.
8. LINDQUIST, ELMER F.: *Design and Analysis of Experiments in Psychology and Education.* Boston, Houghton Miffin Co., 1956,
   pp. 47-100.
9. LINKS, ELEANOR: *A Comparison of Two Methods of Using Radio
   in the Changing of Certain Social Attitudes,* unpublished
   Master's thesis, State U. of Iowa, 1945.
10. MACCOBY, E. E., and WILSON, W. C.: Identification and observa-
    tional learning from films. *J. Abnorm. Soc. Psychol., 55*:76-87,
    1957.
11. MERTENS, MARJORIE S.: *The Effects of Mental Hygiene Films on
    Self-Regarding Attitudes.* Technical Report SDC 269-7-22.
    Washington, D. C., Dept. of Commerce, Office of Technical
    Services, 1951.
12. OSGOOD, CHARLES E., SUCI, GEORGE J., and TANNENBAUM, PERCY
    H.: *The Measurement of Meaning.* Urbana, U. of Illinois Pr.,
    1957.
13. OSGOOD, CHARLES E., and TANNENBAUM, PERCY H.: The principle
    of congruity in the prediction of attitude change. *Psychol. Rev.
    62*:42-55, 1955.

14. RAMSEYER, L. L.: *A Study of the Influence of Documentary Films on Social Attitudes,* unpublished Ph.D. dissertation, Ohio State U., 1939.
15. RATHS, L. E., and TRAGER, F. N.: Public opinion and crossfire. *J. Educ. Socio., 21*:345-60, 1948.
16. ROSENTHAL, S. P.: Change of socio-economic attitudes under radical motion picture propaganda. *Arch. Psychol., 25,* April, 1934.
17. RUBIN-RABSOM, G.: Ease in affecting shift. *J. Soc. Psychol., 31*: 151-54, 1950.
18. SCHLORFF, P. W.: *An Experiment in the Measurement and Modification of Racial Attitudes in School Children,* unpublished Ph.D. dissertation, New York U., 1930.
19. SCOLLON, ROBERT W.: *The Relative Effectiveness of Several Film Variables in Modifying Attitudes: A Study of the Application of Films for Influencing the Acceptability of Foods.* Technical Report SDC 269-7-60. Washington, D. C., Dept. of Commerce, Office of Technical Services, 1956, p. 21.
20. SUCI, GEORGE J.: *A Multidimensional Analysis of Social Attitude with Special Reference to Ethnocentrism,* unpublished Ph.D. dissertation, U. of Illinois, 1952.
21. TANNENBAUM, PERCY H.: *Attitudes Toward Source and Concept as Factors in Attitude Change Through Communications,* unpublished Ph.D. dissertation, U. of Illinois, 1953, p. 28.
22. THURSTONE, L. L., and PETERSON, R.: *Motion Pictures and the Social Attitudes of Children.* New York, Macmillan Co., 1933.
23. WIESE, M., and COLE, S. G.: A study of children's attitudes and the influence of a commercial motion picture. *J. Psychol., 21*: 151-71, 1946.
24. WILLIAMS, DOROTHY M.: *A Study of the Relative Effectiveness of Selected Teaching Procedures in the Modification of Children's Attitudes Toward the Negro,* unpublished Ph.D. dissertation, New York U., 1946.
25. WILLIS, EDGAR E.: *The Relative Effectiveness of Three Forms of Radio Presentation in Influencing Attitudes,* unpublished Ph.D. dissertation, U. of Wisconsin, 1940.

Chapter 17

RETENTION OF THE EFFECT OF ORAL PROPAGANDA

WILLIAM KEH CHING CHEN

Columbia University

THE PROBLEM

Propaganda has repeatedly been found effective in shifting one's attitudes, opinions, or judgments. But how permanent is the effect?

Thurstone[2] measured the retention of the effects of motion pictures upon children's attitudes. He reports that attitudes shifted back about half way toward their original positions in four months. Yet in one group the effect was completely retained for five months.

PROCEDURE

The present study attempted to find out the amount of retention of the effect of ten to fifteen minutes of oral propaganda. The original effects are reported elsewhere.[1] Use was made of the attitudes of American college students toward the Manchurian problem. The first test was given in November, 1932; the second test two weeks later, immediately after the propaganda talk; and the third test in May, 1933. The third test was originally scheduled to be given in March, but postponed owing to the first-page news of Japan's invasion of Jehol. The three tests consisted of exactly the same statements of opinions or attitudes. The first test measured the original attitude; the second, the effect of propaganda; and the third, the retention of the effect of propaganda. The scores were based upon 20 statements of opinion on the Manchurian problem.[1]

Note. Reprinted by permission from *The Journal of Social Psychology*, 7:479-483, 1936.

Each statement was checked on a five-point scale as *A T* (absolutely true). *PT* (probably true, or more true than false), *D* (in doubt, divided, open question), *PF* (probably false, or more false than true), or *AF* (absolutely false). The answer indicating a pro-Japanese attitude was scored as five, the pro-Chinese answer was scored as one. Answers between these extremes were scored two, three, and four respectively.

The second test was given immediately after presentation of oral propaganda material. Significant shift of attitudes was found and proved to be due to the propaganda material itself, not simply due to the personalities of the speakers. The significant difference between attitudes as tested on the first and second tests far surpassed the differences as shown in the nonpropaganda or "control" groups.

The third test was introduced five and one half months later, to measure the prolonged retention of the effect of propaganda. The data presented here are based upon two groups of Columbia students. For the sake of convenience, they are indicated by *CJ* and *CC*. The former designate the Columbia group exposed to pro-Japanese propaganda, and the latter the other Columbia group which was given pro-Chinese propaganda (Table 17-I).

Evidently attitudes, as registered on the third tests by both groups, tend to return to their original positions. In both groups, the differences between the first and third tests are not statistically

TABLE 17-I

Groups Tests	1st	CJ 2nd	3rd	1st	CC 2nd	3rd
N	59	59	28	80	80	52
M	46.03	53.62	48.86	46.88	39.75	46.50
σ	9.20	11.35	7.55	10.00	9.76	11.34
$\dfrac{D}{\sigma D_{12}}$		5.13			9.14	
$\dfrac{D}{\sigma D_{13}}$		1.99			.36	
$\dfrac{D}{\sigma D_{23}}$		3.03			6.43	

Note. The higher the score, the more nearly the subject accepts the Japanese attitude.

TABLE 17-II

Average Difference Between	Statement Nos. Significantly Influenced in the CC Group							
	7	10	22	23	24	33	34	38
1st and 2nd tests	−.44	−.23	−.60	−.35	−.64	−.64	−.66	−.41
1st and 3rd tests	.17	.06	−.47	−.15	−.03	−.12	−.02	−.39
2nd and 3rd tests	.61	.29	.13	.20	.61	.52	.64	.02

significant (D/σ$_D$'s=1.99, .36), but those between the second and the third are significant (D/σ$_D$'s=3.03, 6.43) and between the second and first are significant (D/σ$_D$'s=5.13, 9.14). In other words, the average attitude as measured on the third test is more like that expressed on the first test than like that on the second test. So far as total score is concerned, the effect of both propaganda talks nearly disappeared after the five and one half months' interval.

Table 17-II shows that a few statements still show retention of the effect of propagnada. As reported elsewhere,[1] there were some single statements very significantly affected by the propaganda. Statement no. 24, for instance, showed a minus or pro-Chinese shift of .64 on a five-point scale from the first to the second test. But on the third test it showed only a minus shrift of .03 from its mean on the first test. Comparing the second and the third tests, it may be said that there was a shift of .61 of a step back to the original attitude before propaganda. Only statements nos. 22 and 38 in the *CC* group (Table 17-II) and no. 19 in the *CJ* group (Table 17-III) show no marked difference on the third test from the second.* This suggests retention of the effects of propaganda in these few cases.

TABLE 17-III

Average Difference Between	Statements Nos. Significantly Influenced in the CJ Group						
	1	14	10	17	19	28	34
1st and 2nd tests	58	.68	.69	.59	.41	.57	.81
1st and 3rd tests	.19	.14	.03	.17	.33	.25	.22
2nd and 3rd tests	−.39	−.58	−.66	−.43	−.08	−.32	−.59

*No. 22. "China does not respect the treaty rights of Japan in Manchuria."

No. 38. "The Chinese government should suppress anti-Japanese boycott in China."

No. 19. "Japan is justified in using her power to gain control over Manchuria because Mauchuria possesses raw materials which are important for the development of Japanese industries."

TABLE 17-IV

Quintiles	Quintiles in the CC Group				
	1	2	3	4	5
Difference between 1st and 2nd tests	2.35	—3.50	—6.77	—9.80	—14.80
Difference between 1st and 3rd tests	6.57	—2.06	—3.00	—3.81	— 0.98

The total shifts of different individuals from the first to the second test were arranged according to size and grouped into quintiles in facilitating our comparison. As shown in Tables 17-IV and 17-V, four quintiles shifted with the propaganda (minus or pro-Chinese shift in *CC,* and plus or pro-Japanese in *CJ*). The first quintile in *CC* and the fifth quintile in *CJ* shifted in a direction opposite to that intended by the propaganda. The four quintiles which were affected as intended show a return to their original positions (i.e. the deviations from test 1 are less on test 3 than on test 2). The quintile which reacted in a direction opposite to that expected shows, in both cases, an *increased* deviation from their original position. For instance, in the *CC* group, the fifth quintile made a plus or pro-Japanses shift of 2.35 in spite of the pro-Chinese propaganda. After a lapse of about five and a half months, it showed an even greater pro-Japanese shift. This group of individuals seems to offer resistance to the pressure of propaganda, and later, long after the propaganda, it shifts still more in the opposite direction, or reacts negatively with even more momentum.

CONCLUSIONS

The present study seems to justify the following conclusions:

1. With a lapse of about five and a half months after a ten to fifteen minute propaganda talk, the international attitudes of college students tend to swing back to their original positions.

TABLE 17-V

Quintiles	Quintiles in the CJ Group				
	1	2	3	4	5
Difference between 1st and 2nd tests	19.40	12.85	6.87	4.25	—2.46
Difference between 1st and 3rd tests	9.12	4.82	4.86	2.57	—3.50

2. However, the effect of propaganda upon a few statements may be retained after this period.

3. Those who apparently react against propaganda show greater negative after effects of propaganda after the five and one half months' interval.

REFERENCES

1. CHEN, W. K. C.: The influence of oral propaganda material upon students' attitudes. *Arch. Psychol.,* No. 150, p. 43, 1933.
2. THURSTONE, L. L.: The measurement of social attitudes. *J. Abnorm. Soc. Psychol., 26*:249-269, 1932.

Chapter 18

THE INFLUENCE OF INFORMATION ON THREE DIMENSIONS OF PREJUDICE TOWARD NEGROES

Louise E. Merz and Leonard I. Pearlin

Cornell University   Ohio State University

The underlying thesis of this paper is that a multidimensional analysis of attitudes, in contrast to a monolithic treatment, can lead to a more precise understanding of their development and modification. Prejudice, it is felt, can be taken as a case where the utilities of a multidimensional approach can be shown. To demonstrate this, prejudice toward Negroes was specified into some of its component parts or dimensions; following this, the relationship of information concerning Negroes to each of the specified dimensions was observed. The results of these procedures are reported below.

SPECIFICATION OF THE CONCEPT OF PREJUDICE

Prejudice toward Negroes is treated here as an attitude and, like any other attitude, it is a "persistent, general orientation . . . toward the environment."[1] In addition, it is viewed as a multidimensional phenomenon rather than as a single, unitary entity.

Several social scientists suggest such a multidimensional approach to the study of prejudice. Williams[2] states that a consideration of prejudice as a "blanket concept covering a variety of concrete phenomena is more valid than a consideration of prejudice

Note. Reprinted by permission from *Social Forces, 35*:344-351, 1957. This study was supported financially by a Social Science Research Council undergraduate stipend awarded to Louise E. Merz. Under the arrangements of the grant, Leonard I. Pearlin served as supervisor of the research. The Council assumes no responsibility or control for the research findings.

as a unit." Chein[3] also mentions this approach to prejudice. In their study, Greenblum and Pearlin[4] explain some anomalous data through application of this multidimensional approach. Kramer,[5] too, states that prejudice is composed of many "aspects, categories, or dimensions" and suggests that, in this area, research which considers the various dimensions of prejudice will lead to a more productive understanding of its dynamics. It is his recommendations in particular from which this study borrows heavily.

The dimensions treated by Kramer have been selected for use in this study. They are cognition, emotion, and motivation. Newcomb,[1] Chein,[6] Smith,[7] and Harding *et al.*,[8] also mention one or more of these dimensions.

As they are employed in the present investigation, these dimensions can be defined operationally as follows. Cognition is the ideational dimension of an attitude, including, in this case, the more abstract, analytical thoughts which an individual holds in relation to Negroes. Emotion is the feeling dimension, embracing the presence or absence of generalized upset or disturbance that an individual experiences toward Negroes. Motivation is the action dimension, involving the predisposition of an individual to act discriminately or indiscriminately toward Negroes.

The Establishment and Measurement of the Dimensions

It was discovered early in this investigation that it would be necessary to construct new scales that would permit a separate measurement of each of the three dimensions. A content analysis of existing scales designed to measure prejudice revealed that different items within the same scales embraced the three dimensions as we have defined them; frequently, even the same scale item included more than one dimension. The Guttman scalogram technique, since it works for the unidimensionality of a universe of items, was employed in the construction of the measuring instruments.

Based on suggestions found in the literature, the continuum for each of the dimensions was delimited as follows: (1) cognition, the agreement-disagreement with statements reflecting an individual's more analytical thought processes about Negroes; (2) emotion, the presence or absence of feeling states of disturbance or upset precipitated by inclusion-exclusion of Negroes in social relations of varying degrees of social distance,* and (3) motivation, the predisposition to include Negroes in or to exclude them from social relations of varying degrees of social distance.

A sufficient number of items for each of these scales was gathered so that on the questionnaire there would be at least 12 Guttman-type items for each continuum. Some of these items were taken from existing scales, and others were specially composed. Each item was judged subjectively to determine the dimension on which it lay. From results of a pretest, items were rewritten or discarded whenever necessary and others added.

These items were given as a part of a larger questionnaire to 496 undergraduates in residence at a woman's college.† The subjects were drawn randomly from each of the four college classes. Of the questionnaires distributed, 435 were returned and analyzed.

From the respondents' agreement or disagreement with items, scales were built by utilizing a variation of the Cornell technique.‡ Of the 14 items included on the questionnaire to tap the cognitive dimension, five scaled with a coefficient of reproducibility of .937; of the 12 included to measure the emotional dimension, five scaled with a coefficient of reproducibility of .981; and of the 12 included to test the motivational dimension, five scaled with a coefficient of reproductibility of .956. One-third of the respondents, selected at random, were used in constructing the scales. The other two-thirds were used to check these scales for chance results.

---

*Definition of the emotional continuum in terms of general upset or disturbance resulted from the desire to avoid ambiguity over the meanings which might be attached to terms meant to denote specific emotional states such as love, hate, and so forth.

†It is highly doubtful if the sample in any way vitiates the general implications of the study for a multidimensional conceptualization of attitudes. While this distribution of responses to questionnaire items must be considered appropriate only to the universe from which the sample was drawn, the indicated utilities of a multidimensional treatment of attitudes remain intact.

‡The procedure employed in the scale construction in the present investigation was taken largely from an article by Eric Marder.[9] However, slips of paper were substituted for the metal strips which he recommended. Also, generous assistance was given to the authors in building the scales by Bernard Levin, Department of Psychology, University of North Carolina.

Below are all the items comprising each of the three scales in their final form.

Cognition

1. I believe that in using their influence for their own selfish interests Negroes are threatening the welfare of the entire nation.
2. I believe that the prestige and reputation of the United States as a nation is not impaired by the discrimination of Negroes which exists in this country today.
3. I think that Negroes are getting too much power.
4. Intermarriage between the white and black races, I believe, would cause our society to decay.
5. I believe that Negroes who are insisting on nonsegregated schools are forgetting all the good which the white people have done for them.

Emotion

1. I would be upset if I were to find out that my double date was a Negro.
2. I would be upset if I were to discover that Negroes were staying as guests in the same hotel as I.
3. I would be upset if I were to discover myself sitting beside a Negro in a lecture.
4. I would be upset if I heard that Negroes had been permitted to join my social club.
5. I would be upset if I were to find out that Negroes were patronizing the same dress shops as white people.

Motivation

1. I would do all I could to keep Negroes from sharing the same social position which I hold.
2. I would actively support elimination of segregation of white people and Negroes in all residential areas.
3. I would refuse a job if I found out that my boss were to be a Negro.
4. If I were on a segregated bus and a Negro sat down beside me, I would do all I could to get the Negro to move out of the white section.
5. If a Negro were given membership into my social club, I would withdraw my membership.

After the scales were constructed, subjects were ranked from high to low prejudice on each of the three scales. The ranking was accomplished through assigning each subject to the ideal type which he resembled most closely on each scale. There were six possible ideal types or ranks denoting the amount of prejudice to which a respondent could be assigned. For flexibility in presentation of the results, the first two ideal types were combined to form a rank of "high" prejudice, the second two were combined to form a rank of "moderate" prejudice, and the last two were combined to form a rank of "low" prejudice.

The Relation of Information to the Three Dimensions of Prejudice

Information as a factor in attitude formation and change has been of enduring interest to social scientists. It has often been noted by them that information (or education) is notably ineffective in inducing modification of attitudes.* Despite the rather massive literature on this subject, a great deal remains to be learned. It is a basic assumption of this investigation that an understanding of the influence of information on attitudes in general can be enhanced by a multidimensional view.

One of the first questions to arise was the relative influence of factual information on each of the dimensions. From the existing literature it was predicted that the overall influence of information at most would be slight. Nevertheless, it is pertinent to know if information is differentially related to the specified dimensions. By its very nature, factual information is often relatively free of emotional content. For this reason it was thought that such information would bear more closely on the cognitive and motivational dimensions.

It was not possible to include in the study design a controlled situation where an experimental portion of the sample could be systematically exposed to information favorable to Negroes for a period of time sufficient to bring about an attitude change. Through another means, however, observation of exposure to information was possible. On the questionnaire was an item which asked:

---

*For a summary of much of the work done on the effect of information and education on prejudice see Otto Klineberg, *Tensions Affecting International Understanding* 1950, pp. 126-186.[10]

Do you think that your factual knowledge about Negroes has increased since you have come to College?
Check _____

    _____ A great deal
    _____ A fair amount
    _____ A little
    _____ None
    _____ Don't know

For purposes of presentation the "fair amount" and "little" categories were combined to form a classification of "some" exposure to information. The "don't know" category into which five respondents fell was eliminated here.

This method of determining exposure to information takes the burden from the observer, so to speak, and places it with the respondent. This leaves the way open, of course, for certain selective biases which otherwise might not appear. The results that are presented below, however, suggest that the respondent's appraisal of his exposure conforms sufficiently closely to his actual exposure to allow this question as a measure of exposure to information. The evidence to be used for this contention will be pointed out in some of the data that will be shown below.

Attention now will be focused on the relation of factual information to the three dimensions. First, the answers to the above question are tabulated in Table 18-I with prejudice on the cognitive dimension. This table reveals that as the amount of information to which an individual has been exposed increases, there is a commensurate favorableness on the cognitive level. Thus, the greater the amount of information claimed, the greater the chances

TABLE 18-I

THE RELATION OF EXPOSURE TO INFORMATION FAVORABLE TO
NEGROES TO THE COGNITIVE DIMENSION OF PREJUDICE

Cognitive Dimension	Has Your Factual Knowledge About Negroes Increased?		
	Great Deal	Some	None
	(Percent)	(Percent)	(Percent)
Total	100.0	100.0	100.0
High prejudice	8.9	9.1	13.0
Moderate prejudice	20.2	27.0	36.4
Low prejudice	70.9	63.9	51.6
Number of cases	79	274	77

that one will demonstrate low prejudice. This is clearly illustrated
when it is noted that among those who aver that they received a
great deal of knowledge, 70.9 percent are in the low prejudice
group as compared to 63.9 and 51.6 percent, respectively, of those
responding "some" and "none." There is an association seen here,
then, between exposure to information and relatively low cognitive
prejudice.

However, in the case of the bearing of information on the
emotional dimension, the data show no appreciable or clear link
between these two variables. Table 18-II demonstrates that the
amount of information to which one has been exposed has little
association with the extent of his prejudice on an emotional level.
For example, comparing for the moment only those claiming a
great deal of and no exposure to information, it is seen that there
are no notable differences between these groups with respect to
their proportions displaying high, moderate, or low emotional
prejudice. Interestingly, those who say they have been exposed
to some information elicit more prejudice than either of the other
two groups. These differences, however, are quite small. The data
indicate that there is no significant connection between information and prejudice on the emotional dimension. It might be mentioned in this context that these negative findings can be used to
support our earlier contention that there seems to be no substantial tendency for low-prejudiced respondents to make magnified
claims to greater exposure to favorable information concerning
Negroes. If this did occur, we could expect a closer positive relationship between low prejudice and exposure.

TABLE 18-II

THE RELATION OF EXPOSURE TO INFORMATION FAVORABLE TO
NEGROES TO THE EMOTIONAL DIMENSION OF PREJUDICE

Emotional Dimension	Has Your Factual Information About Negroes Increased?		
	Great Deal (Percent)	Some (Percent)	None (Percent)
Total	100.0	100.0	100.0
High prejudice	12.7	17.9	14.3
Moderate prejudice	39.2	43.1	40.3
Low prejudice	48.1	39.0	45.4
Number of cases	79	274	77

When the relationship between information and motivation is examined, the findings approximate those that were observed for information and cognition. As information concerning Negroes increases, there is a correlative decrease in the disposition to exclude Negroes from social relationships. This is seen compellingly when it is observed in Table 18-III that there are both fewer moderate and more low prejudiced among those claiming a great deal of information than among either of the other two information groups. For example, the proportion of moderate and low prejudiced for those greatly informed are 20.3 and 62 percent, respectively; the corresponding proportions for those stating they have received no information are 41.6 and 46.7 percent.

The preceding data indicate, therefore, that information impinges most directly on the cognitive and motivational levels of attitudes toward Negroes, while exercising little or no influence on the emotional. Since there is no certainty that the classification of prejudice on the three scales manifests precisely the same degree of favorableness or unfavorableness toward Negroes, no rigorous comparisons can be made concerning the relative scores of individuals on each dimension of prejudice. There is sufficient evidence, however, to suggest strongly that the effect of information is not uniform and that monolithic measures of prejudice are not fully adequate in tapping variations in influence.

Conditions Regulating the Influence of Information on the Dimensions of Prejudice

Although it has been demonstrated empirically that some di-

TABLE 18-III

THE RELATION OF EXPOSURE TO INFORMATION FAVORABLE TO NEGROES TO THE MOTIVATIONAL DIMENSION OF PREJUDICE

Motivational Dimension	Has Your Factual Knowledge About Negroes Increased?		
	Great Deal (Percent)	Some (Percent)	None (Percent)
Total	100.00	100.0	100.0
High prejudice	17.7	14.6	11.7
Moderate prejudice	20.3	31.8	41.6
Low prejudice	62.0	53.6	46.7
Number of cases	79	274	77

mensions of prejudice are more sensitive to information than others, there still remains the possibility that there are conditions under which the relationship of information to the various dimensions is strengthened or attenuated. Ego involvement is one such condition.

Ego involvement with an attitude refers to the state where the attitude, identified as part of the self, becomes connected with the maintenance of a given self-image. Under conditions of ego involvement, therefore, it could be expected that there would also be a decidedly greater interest in information concerning Negroes. For this reason, it is predicted that the ego-involved will be more influenced than those not so involved.

The respondents were asked a question which was used as an index of ego involvement. This question is reproduced below.

Do you ever become irritated when you hear people voice their opinions about Negroes which are contrary to yours? Check _____

_____ Always
_____ Very often
_____ Often
_____ Sometimes
_____ Once in a while
_____ Never

The categories of "always" and "very often" were combined to form a category of "strongly" ego-involved. The "often" and "sometimes" designations were joined in a "somewhat" ego-involved category; and the "once in a while" and "never" responses were combined into a category of "slightly" ego-involved.

First the data will be examined to see if ego involvement is a significant condition for the influence of information on cognitive prejudice. For ease and flexibility in presentation, the "great deal" and "fair amount" of exposure to information were condensed into a "most" informed category; and the "little," "none," and "don't know" alternatives were combined to form a "least" informed group.

An examination of Table 18-IV reveals some interesting differences. Perhaps for our purposes the most significant variations occur among the most informed group, for it is this group, it

TABLE 18-IV

THE RELATION OF EGO INVOLVEMENT TO THE INFLUENCE OF
INFORMATION ON THE COGNITIVE DIMENSION OF PREJUDICE

	Information and Ego Involvement					
	Most Informed			*Least Informed*		
Cognitive Dimension	*Strongly Involved*	*Somewhat Involved*	*Slightly Involved*	*Strongly Involved*	*Somewhat Involved*	*Slightly Involved*
	(Percent)	*(Percent)*	*(Percent)*	*(Percent)*	*(Percent)*	*(Percent)*
Total	100.0	100.0	100.0	100.0	100.0	100.0
High prejudice	5.7	8.8	10.1	—	10.3	15.2
Moderate prejudice	14.3	21.1	36.4	35.0	25.3	30.4
Low prejudice	80.0	70.2	53.5	65.0	64.4	54.4
Number of cases	35	114	99	20	87	79

will be recalled, that elicited the lowest cognitive prejudice. Despite their relatively low prejudice, however, some wide differences occur concomitant with the degree of ego involvement. It
should be noted that, of the most informed who are strongly ego-
involved, 80 percent display low cognitive prejudice as compared
to 53.5 percent who are only slightly ego-involved. Even among
those who are least informed similar differences, though not as
large, appear. Thus, the least informed who are strongly involved
more often show low prejudice than the best informed who are
slightly involved. These data suggest that information will be
most effective on a cognitive level under conditions where the
individuals exposed to the information are highly ego-involved.
This is particularly true where such exposure is relatively heavy.

In Table 18-V the same factors are observed in reaction to
prejudice on the emotional dimension. It will be remembered
that no appreciable differences in emotional prejudice were dis-

TABLE 18-V

THE RELATION OF EGO INVOLVEMENT TO THE INFLUENCE OF
INFORMATION ON THE EMOTIONAL DIMENSION OF PREJUDICE

	Information and Ego Involvement					
	Most Informed			*Least Informed*		
Emotional Dimension	*Strongly Involved*	*Somewhat Involved*	*Slightly Involved*	*Strongly Involved*	*Somewhat Involved*	*Slightly Involved*
	(Percent)	*(Percent)*	*(Percent)*	*(Percent)*	**(Percent)**	*(Percent)*
Total	100.0	100.0	100.0	100.0	100.0	100.0
High prejudice	5.7	19.3	21.2	10.0	11.5	17.7
Moderate prejudice	37.1	43.0	44.4	15.0	42.5	46.8
Low prejudice	57.1	37.7	34.3	75.0	46.0	35.8
Number of cases	35	114	99	20	87	79

covered when exposure to information alone was examined. Now, however, compelling differences emerge. An examination of the table reveals, first, that as in the case of cognition, prejudice on the emotional level tends to decrease as ego involvement increases for both the most and least informed. Quite unlike cognition, though, is the fact that ego involvement is most important as a condition when information is light. This can be illustrated by pointing out that among the most informed the proportionate difference between the strong and slightly involved who are low prejudiced is approximately 23 percent, while the difference for their least informed counterparts is about 39 percent. It would appear, therefore, that when a person is both ill informed and strongly involved, the chances are good that he will manifest a relatively high degree of emotional favorableness. Any other combination of exposure to information and degree of ego involvement minimizes these chances. These data suggest that factual information has the consequence of robbing of its emotional quality the attitude with which an individual is ego-involved.

As our final concern we will examine the interplay of information and ego involvement as these bear on the motivational dimension of prejudice. It is seen in Table 18-VI, as might be expected that information is most closely related to favorableness on this level when there is strong ego involvement. Once again, however, suggestive variations are found in these data. Of particular interest is the fact that we find indication that the strongly involved who are least informed are more favorable on the motivational

TABLE 18-VI

THE RELATION OF EGO INVOLVEMENT TO THE INFLUENCE OF
INFORMATION ON THE MOTIVATIONAL DIMENSION OF PREJUDICE

| | Information and Ego Involvement | | | | | |
| | Most Informed | | | Least Informed | | |
Motivational Dimension	Strongly Involved	Somewhat Involved	Slightly Involved	Strongly Involved	Somewhat Involved	Slightly Involved
	(Percent)	(Percent)	(Percent)	(Percent)	(Percent)	(Percent)
Total	100.0	100.0	100.0	100.0	100.0	100.0
High prejudice	5.7	14.0	22.2	20.0	9.2	16.5
Moderate prejudice	25.7	26.4	35.4	5.0	36.8	38.0
Low prejudice	68.6	59.6	42.4	75.0	54.0	45.5
Number of cases	35	114	99	20	87	79

dimension than the strongly involved who are most informed. This seemingly anomalous pattern prompts the conjecture that under certain conditions information, perhaps by creating an awareness of the complexities of an issue, has the latent consequence of inhibiting action on the issue. This has been recognized by Berelson:[11]

> The media atmosphere of public responsibility for public actions may thus become a boomerang; the more the public is enjoined to become an "informed citizenry," the less it feels able to do so. And, overwhelmed by the presentation of issues and problems of a public nature, part of the audience may withdraw into the relative security of their private problems and their private lives.

The empirical evidence above might well be viewed as support for Berelson's statements. These findings are also consistent with those of Hovland and his collaborators* where these researchers demonstrate that knowledge about an issue does not necessarily affect one's willingness to take action on the issue.

SUMMARY AND IMPLICATIONS

It was intended in this paper to demonstrate the utility for research of a multidimensional specification of attitudes. For this purpose, attitudes toward Negroes were selected and conceptualized as being composed of cognitive, emotional, and motivational dimensions. After this, the influence of information on each of the dimensions was observed, both alone and under conditions of varying degrees of ego involvement.

Although it was less the primary purpose to analyze intensively the modification of attitudes by information than to indicate the efficacy of a multi-dimensional conceptualization, several interesting findings emerged. It was evidenced that considered by itself, information has little or no bearing on the emotional dimension. By contrast, there was a fairly close relationship of information to both the cognitive and motivational aspects of prejudice. When ego involvement was introduced as a possible intervening condi-

---

*Hovland and his collaborators found in their studies that while information implements knowledge about an issue, it does not affect action on the issue.[12]

tion for the effectiveness of information, it was discovered that low cognitive prejudice was found most often when an individual was both highly informed and strongly involved. In the cases of the emotional and motivational dimensions, however, it was seen that individuals were more likely to elicit low prejudice under conditions where they are ill informed but highly involved.

Though the above findings leave many questions unanswered, they have some suggestive implications, especially for the assessment of the effectiveness of information campaigns. Probably the most salient point to arise from the data is that information campaigns designed to modify attitudes would achieve greater success if the content of their communications was not only geared to provide more knowledge about the issue, event, or object, but also to generate more interest in the matter per se. Indeed, depending upon the objectives of the campaign, success is perhaps most attainable in achieving a particular balance of factual information and material to arouse ego involvement. The available indications are that if it is action that is ultimately desired, this is begotten not by a saturation of information. To the contrary, relatively little information combined with a relatively high degree of involvement seems most conducive to bringing about a disposition to action.

More work is necessary, of course, before a set of definitive statements can be made of the influence of information on attitudes Sufficient evidence, however, has been reported above to support our major contention that a multidimensional specification of attitudes for research can reveal certain aspects of attitude development and modification which otherwise would be difficult to observe. To the extent that this approach contributes to understanding of attitude modification, social scientists are then in a better position to plan and administer information campaigns, opinionnaires, and future attitude studies.

REFERENCES

1. Newcomb, Theodore M.: *Social Psychology.* New York, The Dryden Press, 1950, pp. 118-119.
2. Williams, Jr., Robin: *The Reduction of Intergroup Tensions: A Survey of Research on Problems of Ethnic, Racial and Re-*

ligious Group Relations. New York, Social Science Research Council, 1947, p. 37.

3. CHEIN, ISIDOR: Some considerations in combating intergroup prejudice. *Educ. Sociol., 19*:412, 1946.

4. GREENBLUM, JOSEPH, and PEARLIN, LEONARD I.: Vertical mobility and prejudice: A socio-psychological analysis. In Reinhard Bendix and Seymour M. Lipset (Eds.): *Class, Status, and Power.* Glencoe, Illinois, Free Press, 1953, pp. 480-491.

5. KRAMER, BERNARD M.: Dimensions of prejudice. *J. Psychol., 27*: 389-451, 1949.

6. CHEIN, ISIDOR: Notes on a framework for the measurement of discrimination and prejudice. In Marie Jahoda, *et al.* (Eds.): *Research Methods in Social Relations,* Part I: *Basic Processes.* New York, The Dryden Press, 1951, pp. 386-387.

7. SMITH, M. BREWSTER: The personal setting of public opinions: A study of attitudes toward Russia. *Public Opinion Quarterly,* 507-523, 1947.

8. HARDING, JOHN, *et al.*: Prejudice and ethnic relations. In Gardner Lindzey (Ed.): *Handbook of Social Psychology.* Cambridge, Addison-Wesley, 1954, vol. 2, pp. 1021-1061.

9. MARDER, ERIC: Linear segments: Technique for scalogram analysis. *Public Opinion Quarterly, 16*:417-431, 1952.

10. KLINEBERG, OTTO: *Tensions Affecting International Understanding.* New York, The Social Science Research Council, 1950, pp. 126-186.

11. BERELSON, BERNARD: Communications and public opinion. In Wilbur Schramm (Ed.): *Mass Communications.* Urbana, U. of Illinois Pr., 1949, pp. 509-510.

12. HOVLAND, CARL I., *et al.*: *Experiments on Mass Communications: Studies in Social Psychology in World War II.* Princeton, Princeton U. Pr., 1949, pp. 255-256.